I0006013

A Fool for His Pains, by Helena Gullifer

A FOOL FOR HIS PAINS.

BY

HELENA GULLIFER,

AUTHOR OF " TRUST HER NOT," ETC.

IN THREE VOLUMES.

VOL. III.

LONDON:

SAMPSON LOW, MARSTON, SEARLE & RIVINGTON,

CROWN BUILDINGS, 188, FLEET STREET.

1883.

CONTENTS OF VOL. III.

CONTENTS.

A FOOL FOR HIS PAINS.

CHAPTER I.

UNPLEASANT REVELATIONS.

THE three ladies sat in comfortable chairs drawn close to the drawing-room fire, with screens to hide their faces from the unbecoming effect of too much heat. Mrs. Torrington was in a dark red satin, which had begun life as a best dress only to be worn on the grandest occasions, and had now descended to a small affair at her brother's house. There were cream-coloured puffings down the front, capitonnés with pearls, and her shoes were of red satin, embroidered in beads to match. Her toilette was the first care of her life, and she would have cried with mortification if anything had gone wrong—such as a pearl fallen out of its puckers, or a hole in the finger of her glove. It had more influence than any amount of moral discourse on her temper;

and she had been known to offend her best friend, if her dress happened to set awry. Unfortunately for Brenda, she had found out that the flounce round the bottom was frayed. Lady Grenville looked quietly aristocratic and good-looking in black tulle, trimmed with lace and jet, and Brenda's pale blue surat was especially becoming to her fairness. Besides the worn-out edge of the flounce, Mrs. Torrington was annoyed with Brenda for being her brother's wife, as well as a prettier and a younger woman than herself, and she meant in a well-bred manner to give her a quiet set down.

Lady Grenville sat between the two, wishing that she could get rid of her gorgeous neighbour, and have a confidential chat with Brenda. The expression of her face had altered so much during the last few days, that her fears were revived as to the wisdom of the marriage.

"I had a visit from Ruthella Chamberlain this afternoon," said Mrs. Torrington, playing with the screen in her hand. "She talked a great deal of your kindness to her in Scotland."

"Indeed. I am sure I don't know what she had to thank me for. I used to think she was rather jealous of my preference for Brenda. Didn't you?" And she turned to Lady Ravenhill, whose eyes were fixed dreamily on the fire.

"Miss Chamberlain! I never thought of it."

"She is not a girl I care for; always rather dull than not, with us women, and sparkling with wit and vivacity as soon as the men came in."

"It is something to find a girl who has wit enough to be amusing when she chooses."

"Yes; but if she does not choose to exert it for my benefit, I don't see why I should care for her."

"Care for her or not, you must confess that she is neither an empty doll," with a look at Brenda, "nor a hardened flirt."

"If she isn't a hardened flirt, she is the most determined young woman I ever saw. She made the most frantic efforts to win your brother's heart;" and Lady Grenville laughed at the remembrance.

"And if she felt an innate consciousness that she was specially fitted to be his wife, I don't blame her. She knew that it would be well for him to marry a girl who had lived all her life in society——"

"Lived all her life? Mr. Chamberlain is nothing in particular."

"And it is just because he can afford to be nothing in particular, that he has the distinction which other men, who work for their living, long for in vain."

"I don't agree with you. There is nothing degrading in work."

"Not perhaps in some work—that of the Prime Minister, for instance."

" Or of a bishop," said Brenda, with a smile.

"No ; there is something respectable about the Church," she said approvingly. " But it is charming to find a man who is nothing, with a mind above all the petty concerns of our daily life."

" Yes, if you don't depend upon him for your daily bread."

"And even if you do, it is so delightful to think it does not cost him the slightest effort. Now, if your father were a solicitor, or a barrister, or anything of that kind," she added vaguely, "it would make the bread taste sour, to think of the trouble it gave him to earn it."

" Do you think so ? " said Brenda, doubtfully, rather too timid with her sister-in-law to air an opinion.

"Yes ; I am not saying it because Mr. Torrington is nothing. Poor man, he is so weak in body that he could not stand the strain on his powers of any sort of work ! But to return to Ruthella ; she would have made such a delightful wife for any—— "

" A member of Parliament, whose mind was incapable of the effort of composing his own speeches," put in Lady Grenville quickly.

Mrs. Torrington looked annoyed. " She told

me all about that wonderful adventure on the lake, Brenda. I did not know before that I owed the inestimable advantage of having you for a sister-in-law, to a night spent alone with Basil, under the most romantic circumstances, on the banks of Loch Allan."

A crimson flush rose over the bride's cheeks. "I don't know what you mean," she stammered.

"Nor do I," said Lady Grenville, with a shrug of her shoulders.

"Well, all I can say is, that it was very fortunate for you that the man was Basil, and that he proposed to you the next day. I've known a girl's character ruined by far less than that."

Lady Ravenhill was about to answer hotly, when Lady Grenville gave her a poke with the point of her shoe, to show that the gentlemen were coming in.

Palpitating with indignation, Brenda rose with undignified haste, and walking hurriedly across the room, turned over the leaves of some music on the piano.

"Are you going to give us a song?" And without looking up, she knew by the tone that Captain Egerton was standing by her side.

"Not now—not yet," she answered tremulously. "Perhaps Mrs. Torrington——"

" She has the voice of a pea-hen. Don't ask her."

" Then Lady Grenville ? "

" She is talking to my brother and your husband, so she must be too happy to wish to be disturbed."

" And I am so hoarse."

He gave a scrutinizing glance at her flushed face. "Play something soft till you have recovered."

She passed her hands over the notes, and a melancholy strain of Schumann's filled the room.

" You don't mind my talking to you, whilst you play ? "

" Not at all."

" Is Raven going to this state dinner in Arlington Street to-morrow ? "

" I believe so."

" And what are you going to do ? "

" Stay at home, I suppose."

" Don't you think it would be more lively to see this new star at the Haymarket ? "

" Infinitely ; but I have no one to take me."

" You forget that I am always at your service."

" Yes, I never thought of you."

" You never do."

" You forget that I got cretonne curtains for my boudoir, on purpose for your cigarette."

"Did you do it for that really?" And in the eagerness of the moment he forgot to drawl.

"On purpose for yours, and other people's."

"Ah, that spoils it."

"Selfish man, did you wish to smoke all alone?"

"I wished the purpose to be for me; the effect might extend to others."

"And perhaps it was," she answered recklessly, almost mad with the pain of her thoughts, as she crushed a loud chord, in the middle of soft variations.

"I am afraid not," said Ronald, with a smile. "You would not tell me if it were."

"I am in the mood for doing or telling anything to-night," she said with energy.

"Then tell me that you will come with me to-morrow evening?" and his own voice was soft as her music.

"Captain Egerton, I am astonished at you;" and much amazed at what she considered his height of audacity, she looked gravely down at her notes.

"Not alone, I never dreamt of that for a moment," he urged, in eager exculpation; "but you have a sister in London, haven't you? Wouldn't she come with you?"

"She might; but she would not care to come without her husband."

"What a devoted wife!" with a light laugh.

"She is quite right," said Brenda, seriously. "If Basil had not been going out, do you think anything would have induced me to leave him?"

"Perhaps not, but then Raven is one in a thousand; and you have not been married seven or eight years."

"How do you know when my sister married?" and she looked up in surprise.

"I judge by the age of that charming little girl I saw at your wedding."

"Ah, I forgot you were there."

"You always do."

"Does it matter if I do? Don't forget *me*, I beg of you, for I shall want every friend I can get in this strange world of London."

He looked at her expressively, began to speak, checked himself, and simply said, "Don't have too many. There is no safety in numbers."

"I should like to know your brother very intimately. His name ought to be Stephen, for I am sure he has the face of an angel. Do you know that I am going to penetrate the darkest recesses of his parish, and find out all the people who are 'sick or sorry'?"

"Then you may find out the whole lot of them; for half are sick, and all of them sorry, except when they are drunk. But promise to

send for me when you act Lady Bountiful, for
you ought not to think of going alone."

"You scarcely look fitted for a district-
visitor," and she laughed softly.

"Marian hopes you will give us a song," said
Lord Ravenhill, sauntering up to the piano,
where Sir Robert soon followed him.

"Certainly, if she wishes it;" and Ronald's
sharp eyes noticed a certain drawing in of the
lips, which generally went in so pretty a curve.

The hoarseness had gone from the rich sweet
voice, and Brenda sang her very best, fired
by the thought that Mrs. Torrington was listening. As the passionate words of a love that
never dies fell from her lips, she raised her eyes
to her husband's face, with all the yearning of
her aching heart in their reproachful glance. It
seemed a relief to pour out her soul, when none
were likely to suspect, and Basil least of all, that
the feeling was anything but the feigned emotion
of a well-taught singer. She could say it all to
him now, though he had married her out of pity,
as she had learned that night. It should be like
the song of the dying swan; she would tell him
once that she loved him with all the passion of
her untrained heart—that he was her lord—her
king—almost her god—and then silence should
bury her love in its oblivion.

"Bravo! bravo!" clapped Sir Robert; but

Ronald was mute, and Lord Ravenhill, even whilst he absently applauded, was wondering, "What is the matter with the child?"

Mrs. Torrington's carriage was announced, and she came forward with a gracious smile to take her leave. "That was really very delightful, Brenda. I had no idea that you sang so charmingly."

"Do I equal Miss Chamberlain?" she asked coldly, as she extended the tips of her fingers.

"Ruthella does not sing, but she plays divinely. —Don't trouble yourself, Basil; I can find my way downstairs alone." In spite of which, he naturally insisted upon escorting her.

"Come and lunch with me as soon as you can," said Lady Grenville, kissing Brenda affectionately. "You don't look quite yourself to-night, but we all have our worries, and I suppose even a happy bride can't be quite exempt. Take care of yourself.—Good night, Captain Egerton.—Good night, Mr. Egerton. Hope we shall see you soon."

Cuthbert politely offered her his arm, although Sir Robert was there, ready to see his wife into the carriage.

Brenda walked to the fireplace. Ronald followed.

"Are you still of the same mind as to the theatre, to-morrow, Lady Ravenhill?"

" Certainly. Why should I have changed ? "

" Oh, I don't know. Half an hour is rather a long time for a woman to be without changing."

" I should like to go, if my sister can come with me. But then how shall I let you know in time ? "

" I shall get the tickets anyhow; for if Mrs. Hayward fails, somebody else is sure to turn up, and I will call in the afternoon to see if I have to hunt up a chaperone."

" I am sorry to give you so much trouble."

" I don't mind it much," he answered with a smile, as he stooped to pick up a small eucharis lily, which had fallen from the front of her dress. " May I keep it ? It might almost count as treasure-trove."

She stretched out her hand for it ; but, as she did so, the sight of the flower reminded her of the one that M. de Biron gave her, as he said, " Revenge him by the future," and her arm fell. The next moment it was too late to recall it, for its pure white star shone from Ronald's coat, and the two others came back into the room.

There was a little talk about the arrangements for to-morrow, of which Lord Ravenhill approved, and then the brothers withdrew, Captain Egerton refusing the charms of the smoking-room, as Cuthbert was anxious to get back to some " ridiculously pampered pauper."

"Since this last attack he has never been able to get to sleep," he said, wishing to exculpate himself from the charge of over-indulgence, "unless he has some one to read to him."

"Hasn't he got either wife or child?" said Basil.

"Plenty of them—at least, of the children—only Cuthbert spoils him so shockingly;" and, with a laughing look over his shoulder, Ronald hurried his brother downstairs.

CHAPTER II.

THE next morning, directly after breakfast, the second footman was sent to Bryanstone Square with a note to Lady Jemima. After the lapse of an hour, he returned with a heavy parcel, which he carried, according to previous orders, straight to his lordship's study. Basil waited till the door was shut; and then, breaking the seals, discovered the rather shabby desk, which Captain Balfour had tampered with on the night of the arrest. He opened it with the key, which Lady Jemima had remembered to enclose in a bit of paper.

With a mixed feeling of awe and melancholy, he turned over such trifles as small notes and faded flowers, thinking of the poor young fellow to whom perhaps they were still of value, and who had nothing but the sweeter memories of the past wherewith to adorn his cell, barren of even such records as these.

There was a letter from Balfour. He knew
it by the handwriting and the tint of the paper,
in both of which they resembled the letter
which he had received from Lady Trevellyan at
Victoria Station about a fortnight ago. He
drew it from his pocket, and laid the two notes
side by side. The paper of each was of the palest
.buff, and under the flap of either envelope was
printed "F. Robinson, Stationer, High Street,
Bedford." They seemed to possess a curious
fascination for him. He felt as if he had an
important piece of evidence in his hand, and yet
lacked the power to make use of it. He turned
them over; but could tell nothing from the
identity of their size, texture, colour, and watermark. The letter to Flora was a curious production, written in short, terse sentences, as if
the writer were impelled to indite it against his
will.

"Kempstone Barracks, N'. Bedford.

"As the personal friend of Charles Tremayne, I should be glad to help you in any
plan that you may form for his escape. I may
be of more use to you than others, for I am able
to offer you the services of a Romany family,
with whom I am connected. At a word from
me, they will be ready to risk everything to save
Tremayne. They can run like a hare, double
like a fox. If your brother will make the first

start, I can answer for it that the warders shall
be led away on a false scent. You need have no
fear. If they are caught, they can still be of
service with their lies. If they are flogged, it
will do them no harm, for they are used to it.
If you put it off too long, your brother may be
too weak to attempt it. Whatever you do, must
be done *at once.*

"Your obedient servant,

"ANGUS BALFOUR."

"A very good idea! Let him escape to ease
your mind, no matter if he is shot in doing it.
A bullet would silence his tongue better than
anything, and an escape, if successful, would
make it impossible for him to set foot in England for the purpose of clearing his name.
Rather a neat idea to work upon his sister's
mind, with that hint about his failing health.
Faugh! the fellow makes me sick!" and with
an expression of disgust, Lord Ravenhill pushed
the papers aside, and went on with his investiga-
tions. "What is this? Only a receipted bill.
Thirty-five pounds ten and six paid to Mr. Pond
of Bond Street. Foolish young fellow! to go
to the most expensive tailor in London." Just
underneath it was a note in Sir Philip Trevellyan's handwriting. He opened it leisurely;
but ran his eye over it with sudden eagerness,

when he found that it was addressed not to
Charlie, as he had taken it for granted, but to
Balfour. It ran thus :—

"3rd of December,
"Palazzo Chigi, Piazza di Colonna, Rome.

"DEAR CAPTAIN BALFOUR,

"The horse you mention sounds pro-
mising, but the figure is rather high. After the
losses I told you of on the 'Two thousand'
and the Derby, I meant to draw in, and should
prefer a hundred and eighty pounds to two
hundred. If you could manage a reduction of
terms, I should be greatly obliged, and would
pay Mr. Moss a visit shortly, when I run over to
London, as I intend to do for a few days.

"Thanking you sincerely for all the trouble
you have taken,

"Believe me, yours faithfully,
"PHILIP TREVELLYAN."

How did this letter, addressed to Captain
Balfour, get into Charles Tremayne's desk? That
was the question. The "Two thousand" came
in very conveniently as a study for the man who
was about to forge the very words; also the
signature of Philip Trevellyan. Was it a mere
accident that it was placed in close juxtaposition
to the bill signed by Edward Pond? He took
up the bill again, and upon close examination

found that the name on it, though written so indistinctly as to be nearly indecipherable, was certainly not that of Tremayne. It looked like Charles Whittaker; and the habiliments supplied were more fitted for the sea than terra firma, and therefore would not have been ordered by Charlie, who never went out on a yacht, and was not much given to boating. To say the least, the presence of these two papers, Balfour's letter, and Whittaker's bill, supposing the name to be that, was a most curious circumstance. Had the landlady sworn falsely, and did some one—presumably Balfour—gain admittance into Charlie's room, and slip them into his desk through inadvertence, with the rest of the criminating documents? It was a point which deserved the most thorough investigation, and only a lawyer's, or a detective's brain, was fitted to the task. He resolved to seek out Mr. Good-eve, and ask his advice, as he would know more about it than his own solicitor, Mr. Ward, who had not been employed on the case.

Thrusting the other papers back into the desk, he put it safely under lock and key, and, with Trevellyan's note and the stranger's bill in his pocket, left the room. In the hall he met his wife coming towards him, with a letter in her hand.

"Augusta and Herbert will be delighted to

come. Do you think I had better ask them to dinner?"

"Certainly. And I suppose," he answered with a smile, "you wish me to call at the Horse Guards on my way to Lincoln's Inn?"

"Just as you like," with the utmost indifference.

"Why did you give him that flower last night?" he asked suddenly, as he took up his hat. "I didn't mind in the least; but if it had been anybody else than his brother with him, he might have thought it odd."

"It tumbled on the carpet, and he asked for it. Do you object?" And she raised her serious eyes, questioningly. "Because, if so, I had better warn you that Captain Egerton would probably flirt with an old woman of eighty if left alone in her company."

"And so he doesn't mind flirting with a young one of eighteen, who is not so bad-looking as she might be," he said lightly. "Never mind; I can trust Egerton. There is no harm in him. If I am not in time for luncheon, don't wait for me." He nodded pleasantly, as he shut the door behind him.

"'I can trust Egerton!' Flattering to me!" and, with a bitter smile, she turned away. "If Flora Trevellyan had been his wife, he might have cared sufficiently to be jealous."

Lord Ravenhill, perfectly unconscious of the storm he left behind him, walked briskly through the narrow opening into Constitution Hill, enjoying the freshness of the frosty air and the evanescent brightness of the sun. He thought much of Brenda, as he went along the Mall, wondering why she had grown so much graver during the last few weeks, than she was at Paris or Nice, why she looked at him so pathetically when she was singing that fervent song, as if he had been a second Bluebeard, and she had just discovered his murdered wives. There was no doubt that she loved him; he could read it in her eyes, even when she shrank from him, as she seemed to do now, whenever he embraced her. Was there something in himself that made it impossible for him to make a woman happy?

He had not solved the problem by the time he reached the Horse Guards. Ronald Egerton was yawning desperately over the morning paper, not having been in bed, in spite of Cuthbert's better example, till the small hours had begun to increase; but he summoned sufficient energy to accept his invitation with pleasure, and declared his willingness to be at Lady Ravenhill's service, at any hour of the day or night.

"And you expect me to deliver such a.

message as that?" Lord Ravenhill asked, amused at his impudence.

"I can tell her so myself, when you are dining in solemn grandeur amongst the solid spirits of the day."

"I wish the solid spirits (if there are such things) at Hanover! I am sure you will have much the best of it."

"I haven't a doubt of it;" and he twisted the tips of his moustaches with a smile.

"Look here, Egerton; I won't have any flirting behind my back."

"I promise to do it just as much before your face."

"Humph!" with a shake of the head. "I believe I shall have to forbid you the house, and get your brother to come in your stead."

"If you do, Lady Ravenhill will turn into a Sister of Charity before a month is up; and instead of stalls at the opera, she will drag you to a cramped-up seat at Exeter Hall!"

"Heaven forbid! Well, I mustn't wait. If I can get away in time, perhaps I shall join you."

"Pray don't hurry on my account," drawled Ronald, as he threw himself back in his chair.

"Incorrigible fellow!" said Basil to himself, with a smile, as he crossed Parliament Street on his way to the Strand.

CHAPTER III.

A CAUTIOUS MAN.

"Stop a bit," said Goodeve, taking off his spectacles to wipe them with his silk handkerchief. "I have a paper locked up in this drawer, which I think may be of some use, after all."

"What is this?" asked Lord Ravenhill in some surprise, as the solicitor took out a sheet of paper and spread it on the table, with a smile of superior wisdom.

"One of the criminating documents produced at the trial of Charles Tremayne. It would have been thrown away with the rest, only St. John had scribbled such a capital likeness of Baron Brown on the back, that I slipped it into my pocket. Do you notice anything particular about it?"

Ravenhill turned it backwards, forwards, and upside down. "I never saw Brown, so I am no judge as to the likeness; but I can see that the paper is just the same tint as Balfour's note."

"It is; and that is a most curious circumstance. It is a peculiar colour, and both seem to have come from the same shop. Now, we have no reason for supposing that Tremayne was in the habit of getting his writing materials from Mr. F. Robinson, stationer, High Street, Bedford; but it would be most natural for Captain Balfour to do so, as he has been quartered for some time in the Kempstone Barracks, two miles from the town."

"Yes, but——"

"Excuse me, my lord. I wish to put this plainly before you. If these attempts at copying Sir Philip Trevellyan's handwriting are written on Balfour's paper, it seems to me presumptive evidence that they were written in his rooms, if not by his hand. If so, the fact would prove him to be an accomplice; and if we can once do that, it would not be so hard a matter to prove that he was the principal;" and he brought his hand down with a thump on the table, as he looked into Lord Ravenhill's eager eyes.

"You don't say so!" he exclaimed, as if the idea were new to him.

"Once destroy the idea that Balfour is absolutely innocent, and you expose him to the suspicion of absolute guilt. Cannot you see it for yourself? By his own confession, he was alone in the room with Sir Philip's cheque-book, before Tremayne came in. He says that he left it before my client's visit; but I think the evidence to prove this was weak. It was taken for granted, because a footman had not heard him go down the stairs; but as it was never suggested that he went out of the window, and therefore must have come down through the hall, either before or after, this proves nothing. Let us look at the watermark on the two papers, and see if they agree."

They both rose, and went to the window. In consequence of the writing on either side, the marks were hard to decipher, but they fancied that they could trace a resemblance between them.

"Then you think there is a chance of clearing Tremayne?"

"Not the slightest;" and the lawyer shook his grey head.

Lord Ravenhill, taken aback, opened his eyes.

"For my part, I cannot see a loophole. If he is not the principal, he *must* be an accomplice; and although we might get a mitigation of his sentence, the result would none the less be social ruin."

"Then you refuse to undertake the case?"

"Certainly not. When I *see* a case, I shall be happy to take it up."

There was a pause, whilst both were busy with thought.

Mr. Goodeve's eyes wandered to a tin case, in which he had secreted the letters which Captain Balfour had returned on his application. They were not burnt as Charlie had directed, for the shrewd lawyer suspected that they held the secret of his client's obstinate silence. As they were written by Lady Trevellyan, he felt bound in honour not to show them to any one, but to reserve them till he could place them in the writer's own hands. At the same time, he was afraid of sending them to Rome, for one glance at their contents had shown him that they were of a compromising character, and might consequently bring about a difficulty with her husband.

"If Tremayne had not actually spent some of the money," said Lord Ravenhill, slowly, "I think we might have got over everything else."

"But he did," said Mr. Goodeve, rubbing his chin.

"If we could only prove that he had borrowed it innocently."

"But we can't."

"I know it," said Basil, irritated at the

solicitor's evident contempt for his suggestions; "but I don't despair. And I mean to clear Tremayne, if I spend my last farthing in the effort."

Mr. Goodeve's small eyes twinkled knowingly. "Mr. Tremayne has the advantage of possessing a most generous, and disinterested friend."

Basil assumed an expression of haughty reserve, and answered coldly, "I should be sorry to forget a man directly he got into trouble."

"You do rather more than not forget him, my lord; you remember him to some purpose."

"I intend to."

"Am I at liberty to retain these two papers?" taking up Balfour's note, and the tailor's bill.

"If you will. They may be safer in your hands than in mine. I suppose it would be a good thing to have a watch put on Balfour's movements?"

"I don't see much use in it, unless it could help us to find out if he has opened an account at a fresh bank."

"If he increased his expenses, that would prove something."

"He has got the two thousand required for his bride's settlements. I suppose the next thing will be that they will marry. They would not be able to launch out much, with only ninety to a hundred added to their yearly income."

"But the two thousand, I presume, would be tied up."

"I was thinking of the four."

"Ah! Then you are as much convinced of his guilt, as I am."

"It would take positive proof to convince me," said the wary solicitor.

"Then we must find it," said Basil, with a smile. "I am going to turn myself into an amateur detective for the first time in my life; and when I have done all I can, I shall come back to you, and get you to make something of the materials which I hope to furnish." He got up, and extended his hand. "Good morning."

"I have not much opinion of amateur work, as a rule," said Mr. Goodeve, shaking hands; "but nothing would please me better than your success. Good morning, my lord." He bowed him out, then returned to his fire to ruminate.

With a ponderous shake of his head, he sat down in his comfortable armchair. "I should be sorry to think badly of Tremayne's daughter, but it looks queer, to say the least. His name was on those letters, with a very warm expression attached to it; and then, why should he come and meddle in the case, if there weren't some special reason at the bottom of it? The affair is mine, not his, and I mean to work it on my own lines, without taking instructions from outsiders. The Trevellyans can pay me if they choose, but I am not going to touch *his* money for the help I give to a Tremayne. For his father's sake I would do the best I could for the poor fellow, who seems to have been the greatest idiot that God ever made." And with this conclusion he wound up his reflections, and rang for his clerk.

CHAPTER IV.

"THAT'S THE MAN!"

"What do you think of Captain Egerton?" inquired Mrs. Hayward of her husband, as she poured out the tea at breakfast the following morning.

"Delightful! What could be more charming than his way of listening to a woman's words, and supplying her wants, before she is aware of them herself?"

"Nonsense! I want to know your real opinion of him as a man."

"As a man? Humph! I never regarded him as anything else;" and he slowly buttered a piece of toast. "He must have something in him, or he would not be attached to the Intelligence Department at the Horse Guards; and he certainly has something outside him, or women would not care to look at him so much."

"I don't want to know what is thought of

him by women or soldiers. What do you think of him, yourself?"

Mr. Hayward took up the *Times*, and pushed his cup across the table for a fresh supply. "If I were a bachelor, I should like him to live next door. As the husband of a pretty wife, the west coast of England would scarcely be far enough."

Augusta blushed. Conjugal compliments *are* such a treat. "Ah, I thought as much;" and she gave an oracular shake of her head. "Brenda is a great deal too flighty in her manner for a married woman."

"Poor child! I never said so," said Mr. Hayward, hastily. "She is too young, too pretty, and too inexperienced, to have a fair chance at the first start, that is all."

"Brenda is nice-looking, but I don't call her lovely because she has developed into a peeress."

"Nor do I; but I expect she developed into a peeress because she was lovely," said her husband, drily.

"Stuff and nonsense! Really the way in which men rave about her is enough to turn her head."

"But, at any rate, not to turn her heart. Did you see the look she gave her husband the moment he came in?"

"Yes; but she had been whispering to Captain Egerton just before, and missed the best point of the play."

"So long as her heart is in the right place, you needn't pull such a long face."

"It makes me very uneasy," said Augusta, bridling up. "As her eldest sister, I feel in some way responsible for her actions."

"Good gracious! With a husband to look after her, I don't think she need add a feather-weight to your mind."

"If I feel it my duty, I shall remonstrate."

"Do nothing of the kind. A simple word may turn a frank friendship into something infinitely worse."

"It might stop it, on the contrary."

"Not a bit of it. Your sister's own good sense will do that. Remember, she is very young, and let her have her fling."

"In other words, I am to let her flirt with every man that comes to the house."

"Leave her to Ravenhill. From what I gather of his character, he is not likely to be too indulgent. And, you know, my dear," he added with a smile, as he took up his hat and brushed it with his coat-sleeve, "those who interfere between husband and wife make a hole in the peace, and add much to the strife. Good-bye." He brushed her cheek with his whiskers—a conjugal scrub which somehow seems to give pleasure to a wife—and with a cheerful nod to his little daughter, left the room.

Mrs. Hayward sighed, as was her wont, and then, catching sight of Mabel in the act of helping herself to half the marmalade, she told her sharply not to dawdle over her breakfast, and locked the jam, etc., up in the cellaret. Thus having secured her daughter from further temptation, she proceeded to study the births, deaths, and marriages in the *Times*.

Later in the morning, she thought she would relieve her mind by giving a word of advice to Brenda, in spite of her husband's counsel; for Mrs. Hayward was prone to great anxiety about the affairs of others, and seemed to be pricked by her too active conscience when other people failed to fulfil their duties. It was not enough for her to look after her own; she must keep her eye on her sister's as well. But when she reached Grosvenor Place, she was told that her ladyship had gone down to Inglefield; so she returned home, with all her words of wisdom left unsaid.

Brenda, meanwhile, was seated in the midst of her family, and any one to look at her bright face would have thought there was not a cloud on her happiness. It was good to be with them once again, to have them round her, listen-

ing in rapt attention to every word she said,
and gazing with fond admiring eyes at her
splendours. Her poor bruised heart felt soothed
into peace as she sat with her mother's hand
in hers, and Mary and Edith stitching close
beside her.

"Give me something to do. I shan't feel
really at home, without a thimble on my finger."
And, in spite of all remonstrance, she took a
skirt, the seams of which had to be run, out
of Mary's hand, and set to work with great
diligence. "You remember how I used to hate
work when I had to do it, and now it is quite
a treat."

"We will send you up a parcel by the
carrier," said Edith; "and won't your grand
footmen stare when they walk in to find her
ladyship turned into a dressmaker?"

"Not at all. A great many grandees make
petticoats and things for the poor; and I could
give out that I was supporting a widow and her
family by my needle;" and Brenda laughed
merrily.

"I would rather you supported us by your
tongue," said Mary, with a quiet smile.

"Why?"

"Because it is sure to work the hardest."

"For shame! I did not come home to be
insulted. Oh, mother dear, do you know, I am

going to be presented next Wednesday, and I
feel in such a fright. Fancy if I fell down
when I made my curtsy! It would never be
forgotten.''

"But why should you?" said her mother,
sensibly. "You are not more awkward than
other people."

"No; but a cousin of Captain Egerton's
did, and she was called 'the fallen angel' for
the rest of the season."

"But there is nothing angelic about you,
Bren, so be comforted," remarked Edith, as she
stopped to thread her needle.

"That won't prevent me from tumbling."

"No; but it will save you from such a nick-
name. What is your garment to be?"

"Oh, something very gorgeous from Élise.
You shall see it when you come up. People
are so kind to me. Two or three have already
asked to be allowed to present me with my
bouquet."

"And which is the favoured one?"

"Captain Egerton. He does everything for
me in the most good-natured way. Augusta
does not like him for some reason or other, and
when she went to the Haymarket with us, she
was barely civil. But you know how full of
whims she is."

"Yes; if you are not in high favour she

treats you like a convict. There is no betwixt and between;" and Mary got up to ring the bell for luncheon.

"I left a few parcels in the hall," said Brenda, with a smile. "Perhaps you had better go and look at them."

There *were* a few parcels indeed! Heaps of little delicacies, most suited to her mother's and sisters' fancies, were brought in and rejoiced over. The tears came into Brenda's eyes, as she was hugged and kissed, again and again. There was some comfort for her in life so long as she could come down laden with gifts, like a beneficent goddess, to her own home. As she sat at the little luncheon table, with her eyes fixed on the waterfall in the garden, she asked herself if she would change if she could, and be Brenda Havergel once more? And, without hesitation, she answered "No." On the path which she was travelling, whatever the grief and the sorrows, there could be no thought of going back. It was better, far better, to belong to Lord Ravenhill, to form part of his life and his future, than to sink into the nothingness of her former existence, and be the girl whom he had liked and forgotten. Rousing herself from her abstraction, she asked suddenly—

"What about Mr. Ward? you have not mentioned him for a long while."

"He was dining here the night before last," said Edith; "and his daughter Kate is going to be married next week to Captain Balfour."

"What day?"

"Friday, I think—at St. Pancras's, Euston Square."

"I have heard so much of him lately. He figured in a forgery case, and not greatly to his advantage. People said it turned their blood cold to hear him giving evidence against a man who had been his best friend."

"What a disgusting creature! Mamma, don't you remember that you always fancied that Mr. Ward disliked him?"

"Yes, Edith. But he said it would have broken Kate's heart if he had forbidden the match. She seems to be quite infatuated about him."

"So was Charlie Tremayne, the poor fellow who got into trouble. I should like to see the wretch, if only for the sake of satisfying my curiosity. Edith, you shall go with me. You are coming to stay with us, you know. Basil sent you a polite message to the effect that he would be delighted to see you. What with the House, and other engagements, I really see very little of him, so it would be a charity to take pity on me."

Edith's eyes danced with pleasure. "But,

Brenda, you will be so frightfully gay, and all
your friends are such swells."

"Lent is just beginning, so we shall be rather
dull, on the contrary; but we can go to all your
pet churches, and hear the best preachers,
according to our original programme.   Will you
come back with me?   I *wish* you would."

"Oh no, I couldn't;" and Edith coloured as
she thought of many drawbacks in her wardrobe.

"Never mind the dresses; I have got enough
for both."

"Next Wednesday—will that do?"

"No; you must come on Tuesday. Wednesday I go to the drawing-room, and you will have
to act as special reporter to mamma."

This was cordially assented to.   Mrs. Havergel's motherly heart swelling with pride at the
thought of the admiration which her child was
sure to excite.

"Brenda dear," she said anxiously, with both
hands laid on her shoulders, in the quiet sanc-
tuary of her own room, "you *are* happy—*quite*
happy?"

"I would not change for the world!" and,
with a sudden burst of tears, Brenda threw her
arms round her mother's neck.

Not long afterwards the carriage was ordered,
and she drove back to town, refreshed by the
loving sympathy of her own people, who never

changed with the changing circumstances of life. It was pleasant to have one sheet-anchor to depend on, in the shifting waters of her present existence ; and she held to it with the tenacity of one who felt that a storm was brewing.

Edith's company did her a great deal of good, and prevented her from brooding over her sorrows, or trying to cure them with dangerous remedies. She endeavoured to bring about a great friend-ship between Bertram Fitz-herbert and her sister ; but the young fellow was so entirely devoted to herself, that it was difficult to persuade him to take even a fractional interest in any one else.

Lady Grenville often dropped in, and always received a hearty welcome ; but she shook her head at the smoking which went on in the pretty boudoir, after calling-hours, and said, "Give a man liberty to do what he likes, and he will do what you don't like, my dear. If he doesn't care sufficiently for you to give up his cigar for your sake, let him go by all means and enjoy it, with-out you, in the smoking-room."

"But Basil likes nothing better than conver-sation and cigarettes. He began it, and the rest naturally follow his lead."

"Ah, if your husband is the culprit, I must hold my tongue. But, remember this as a rule : keep a man under a certain restraint, and he will

like you all the better for it in the end. Respect
is a close companion of restraint, and when
they are both gone, the position is—slightly
embarrassing. What were you doing this
morning? Mr. Vivian told me that he passed
your carriage in Piccadilly, before the lamps
were out."

"What nonsense! We started a little earlier
than usual, because the daughter of our old
friend Mr. Ward was to be married at eleven
o'clock. It was a very quiet wedding. The
bride in white silk and swansdown—only fancy!
The bridesmaids in grey silk and cashmere, with
horrid mobcaps, that used to be the fashion
about three or four years ago."

"Is it a good match?"

"No, as bad as bad can be; but oh! I don't
wonder at it, for he *is* so handsome."

"Who? The bridegroom?"

"Yes, Captain Balfour. Edith fell violently
in love with him."

"Balfour!" exclaimed Lady Grenville, in
surprise. "You mean to say that her father let
her marry a man like that!"

"What has he done?" inquired Edith, whose
indignant denial of special admiration for him
had scarcely been heard.

"Nobody knows. There is a feeling against
him about the Tremayne affair; and they say

that his brother officers have sent him to Coventry."

"There were some very odd people at the church, and I caught sight of a horrid-looking man, who seemed to be hiding behind a pillar. As the bridegroom came up the aisle, he rubbed his hands together, muttering, 'That's 'im; that's the man.' When I looked round, he had slipped out of the pew and was talking to—who do you think?"

"How could I tell? A policeman?"

"No; of all people in the world—Basil!"

"Good gracious!" and Lady Grenville leant forward in sudden interest

"I waited till the end, because I wanted Mr. Ward to know that we were there; and when we got away, he was nowhere to be seen."

"And you have not seen him since?"

"No; he was not coming home to luncheon, so we went down to Eccleston Square. Do you know when the Trevellyans are expected?" she asked, in as careless a tone as she could manage.

"About the middle of April, I fancy. Poor thing! I pity her so dreadfully. Brenda, you and she must be great friends."

"I don't see a chance of it;" and she pursed up her pretty lips with an air of reserve.

"But, Brenda!" exclaimed Edith, who knew

nothing of the *arrière-pensée*, "I thought every
one said she was quite irresistible."

"And so she is—to men; but that is no
reason why women should worship her as
well."

"I did not talk of worship," said Lady
Grenville gently, all her fears revived by the
bitterness with which Brenda spoke. "I
always looked upon her as a woman whom it
would be quite a privilege to call my friend;
but they have lived so much abroad that we
meet too seldom for anything beyond acquaintance."

"I shall be quite satisfied without anything
more. To-morrow afternoon," she added quickly,
in order to turn the subject, "Bertie Fitz-
herbert, your nephew, Mr. Grenville, and Captain
Egerton, are coming to escort us to the Grosvenor
gallery. They say the collection there is something extraordinary; and there is a wonderful
likeness of Mrs. de Vaudeville at a shop a little
lower down. I wish you would join us?"

"Impossible; I wish it weren't. But this
life cannot be all pleasure, as you young people
seem to fancy. There are a few duties to be
done."

"Pleasure?" interrupted Brenda. "Life
seems made up of everything else.

"Not *your* life, Bren," said Edith, thinking

of all the home troubles which she had escaped
by her marriage.

"Why not mine?" she asked resentfully, as
the colour flew to her cheeks. "Am I the
happiest of mortals because I live in a big house,
and have no chance of starving?"

"Any woman in good health—for a simple
toothache may make you wretched—who has a
charming house, a good fortune, and an almost
faultless husband, stands in the position of Poly-
crates the Fortunate, who threw his favourite
ring to the gods, in order to avert their dis-
pleasure at his godlike fate. What will you
throw, Brenda?"

"My heart; and see if any one cares to pick
it up."

"It is forbidden to throw away your husband's
property. Miss Havergel, your sister seems to
have strange notions as to *meum et tuum.*
Pray read her a lecture as soon as my back is
turned. I know it is the favourite practice of
younger sisters."

CHAPTER V.

THE OLD LOVE AND THE NEW.

" PUT on the prettiest dress you have, Brenda,"
said Lord Ravenhill, as he came into his wife's
boudoir, about five o'clock one lovely afternoon
in early May, and threw himself down on a sofa
close beside her chair. "I want you to look
your very best to-night, and out-rival every other
star."

She looked up at him; her face flushed with
pleasure, though she only said, "I feel as if it
would be hopeless to try."

"Do you? Then you are sure to succeed;
ugly women are always the most conceited."

"And I thought you never cared about a
woman's dress."

"What an absurd idea! If you had ever
ventured to look dowdy, I should soon have put
in a remonstrance."

"If you had time to notice it; but you are
always so busy now. Shall I give you some
tea?"

"Please. I always have time to notice any-thing and everything about my wife," he said gravely. "For instance, I know that for the last few weeks, at least, she has not seemed to care for me as she did when we first married."

She stopped in the act of handing him his teacup, her hand shaking so violently that the beautiful Sèvres china would probably have fallen, if he had not taken it from her.

"I don't know how you can think so," she faltered.

"Well, I find that you would rather talk to any one but me; that you turn white or red if ever I meet your eye, as if I were something rather unpleasant to look at."

"Basil!"

"I only judge by your evident wish to look another way. If we dine alone together, you are almost silent, whilst if any one drops in, like Egerton, for instance, you can chatter as you used to do when I first knew you."

"And perhaps you think I like him better than you?" she asked, her bosom heaving, her lips trembling.

"God forbid! It would be hard indeed if you could not be true to me for four or five months. All I want to know is, what I have done to produce such a change in you? If I am in the wrong, pray tell me, and I will try to get

myself right again. Perhaps you are offended
with me because I can't go out with you always,
as I did at Nice; but you must remember I was
having a holiday then, and now my working
days have begun. There is a question at present
before the House which is of vital importance,
and it would take a great deal to keep me away
from the debates; also I have many affairs to
attend to, connected with committees, etc.,
which you would not understand, but which give
me plenty of things to do. And, besides all
these hindrances, there is yet another;" and he
fixed his earnest eyes upon her upturned face.
"I thought, rightly or wrongly, that you no
longer cared for my escort."

The colour came and went in her cheeks, her
eyes looked piteously into his; she tried to be
calm and indifferent, but nature was too strong
for her. Shaking all over, she looked down into
her lap.

"If you think our marriage was a mistake,"
he went on gently, misconstruing the cause of
her emotion, "I don't know how to mend it.
It is far easier to tie a knot, than to undo it.
Would it not be better to make the best of a bad
bargain, and bear it with as cheerful a countenance as you can? If I am too old and too serious
for you, I won't say that you ought to have
found it out before, because you were only a

child; and I can't say that I will make myself young again, because that would be impossible, but I have let you surround yourself with younger men, whose liveliness might compensate for any dulness in me, and I have never complained of the coldness you have shown towards myself."

"Because you have never felt it"—came in a smothered voice from close proximity to the tea-tray, over which Brenda was bending.

"Excuse me, I have felt it very much;" and he drew himself up with an air of cold reserve. "What a man feels most, he speaks of least."

"I—thought—you didn't care."

"Then you had no right to. I am not a weathercock to change like—a woman. If you can't love me, you can't, and there's an end of it. I suppose there is something in me which makes it impossible."

"Basil!"

"Well?" He waited. No answer. "I am not blaming you, child, for not caring."

"But I *do!*" and she stretched out her hands with the imploring gesture of a child, utterly unable to resist the voice of her heart any longer.

"No, you don't." He shook his head with an indulgent smile. "You are sorry for me; that is all."

She put up her face, asking for a kiss, as in all her married life she had never asked before; but he only stroked her cheek gently with his hand, thinking the caress was offered as a sop to his injured feelings.

"Basil, won't you believe me? I love you so much, so madly, that I have prayed God to take it from me." Her head was buried on his knees, as she dropped down on the floor beside him.

"And He has answered your prayers?" he said calmly, though his heart beat faster.

"No," in the softest whisper.

He raised her gently from the ground, drew her close to him on the sofa, and encircled her with his arm. "Brenda, don't deceive me, or yourself either. Speak to me now, as before God and your own conscience." She raised her eyes to his, awed and tremulous, looking strangely lovely, in spite of ruffled hair and tear-stained cheeks. "Why do you pretend not to care for me every day of your life, when, in a moment like this, you can say that your love is greater than ever? There must be some reason; if you will tell it me, it may be happier for us both."

She opened her lips to speak; now she would disburthen herself of all the doubts and fears which made her life so miserable. Already she felt relieved of half their weight, when the door opened, and a visitor was announced.

They started apart like a pair of guilty lovers, and welcomed their unwished-for guest with unusual effusion. The moment for explanation passed away, and the fresh air of candour and common sense was not allowed to dispel the shadows of the future.

With a fluttering heart, Brenda allowed herself to be decked in all her splendours for Lady Flutterly's ball. Her husband had expressed a wish for her to look her best; and she was more anxious about her personal appearance this evening than on the day of her Majesty's drawing-room. The *Court Journal* had mentioned her in a flattering paragraph; friends had insinuated their admiration by word or glance; Edith had been unable to restrain her sisterly praise; but Brenda's heart had not beaten with so sweet a throb of vanity as to-day, when Lord Ravenhill expressed an interest in her toilette.

In a lovely cream-coloured dress from Élise, beautiful as it was indescribable, with its puffings and frillings, and laces and fringes, its close-fitting bodice, studied with jewels, and its tiny sleeves, so small as to be almost invisible, Brenda, as desired, looked her very best. She wore nothing in her hair, which was dressed in soft curls on the top of her head, with a small coil of plaits at the back of the neck, and a fluffy fringe on her low white forehead; and nothing round the slender pillar of her throat to mar its graceful outline. The only bit of colour about her dress was a knot of Marshal Niel roses in her bosom. Lord Ravenhill might well be proud of his wife, as he walked into the room by her side; and so absorbed was he by her charms that he actually forgot to remember that evening, years ago, when he stood outside that very door, and waited for Flora Tremayne. And yet the thought of it had kept him from all festivities in Lady Flutterly's house, for five years or more!

"So delighted to see you, dear, looking so charming;" and Brenda's hand was pressed confidingly by her hostess. "The Prince will be here directly, and I promise to introduce you."

"What Prince?" and she looked up at Lord Ravenhill inquiringly.

He shrugged his shoulders. "Only Niederlohe, from the Austrian embassy. The title is everything; the man nothing."

A crowd of friends pressed round them; a highly ornamented card was thrust into Brenda's hand, and several men asked permission to inscribe their names thereon. They were all put off with some excuse. Lady Ravenhill had not made up her mind whether to dance or not, so she moved on, finding that her husband, whose eyes had been searching every part of the crowded drawing-room, was bent upon conducting her to a particular corner. A couple stepped aside, and, without any preparation, she found herself opposite to a lady in black satin, sparkling with jet, and heard her own name mentioned, as Lord Ravenhill introduced her to Lady Trevellyan.

Flora rose, and extended her hand with a winning smile, as she said simply, "I have long wished to meet you."

Brenda gazed at her with startled eyes, as their hands met. Face to face with the far-famed beauty, her own attractions seemed *nil;* and she felt much as the moon might have felt, when introduced to the sun.

This was the reason why she was to look her best, in order that she might appear to advantage in the eyes of Flora Trevellyan! All her pleasurable sensations of gratified vanity vanished in a moment, and, with a bitter sense of personal eclipse, added to the revival of jealousy and doubt, she returned her greeting coldly. Lord Ravenhill looked more annoyed than disappointed, as he introduced Sir Philip, whose eyes were resting with great appreciation on Brenda's graceful figure.

There was an awkward pause. Flora, chilled
by the wife, had too much tact to begin a
conversation at once with the husband; and Sir
Philip, keenly alive to the facts of the situation,
was wondering if Lady Ravenhill's coolness were
the offspring of shyness, or of a deeper feeling
connected with the revived friendship between
his own wife and her husband. It was an
interesting speculation, and for a long minute it
tied his usually fluent tongue.

Ronald Egerton was a welcome interruption
when he sauntered up to the group, and, shaking
hands all round, expressed his surprise and
pleasure at meeting the Trevellyans. One glance
at Lady Ravenhill's face told him that she was
bored or troubled, and, as soon as he could
detach himself from the others, he turned to
her, and said, in a low voice, "Would not a
waltz be the best thing to prescribe for your
complaint?"

"I think it would," she returned, with a
smile, after a first look of surprise. She took
the arm he offered, and he piloted her skilfully
through the throng. She had never liked him
so much before as now, when he rescued her
from a very unpleasant position; and he had
never admired her half so much as this evening,
when her beauty was enhanced by her emotion,
and her dress shone conspicuously amongst

all the splendid toilettes that adorned the
room.

As he passed his arm round her waist, he
looked down at her softly, without a word. How
ineffably charming she was, from those dear little
curls on the top of her head to the tip of her
embroidered shoes, just peeping from beneath
the lace frill at the edge of her dress! "Ravenhill is a lucky man!" he thought, with a smile
and a sigh.

After a few turns, they stopped.

"Your step goes exactly with mine. We
ought to be partners till the end of the season,"
he calmly remarked, as he possessed himself of
her fan.

"There are a few other things to be considered besides a particular step," she said, with
a laughing glance.

"Only a few? Perhaps we might get over
them."

"Too many for that."

"Tell me what they are."

"You know them as well as I do."

"How can you guess how much I know, or
rather, how little?"

"There are some truths which are evident
to all."

"Truths! I've got nothing to do with
them. Society is made up of lies, and I have

lived in society from my earliest years. Take
pity on my ignorance."

"I shall do nothing of the kind; I believe
you are proud of it."

"That is the only way when you have a
defect. I knew a fellow once who was a
hunchback, and he thought it a mark of
distinction."

"Of extinction more likely."

"More likely, but less true. Shall we take
another turn?"

"Not yet. Captain Egerton, what do you
think of Lady Trevellyan?" and she looked up,
with sudden eagerness, into his face.

"What do I think of her?" he said slowly.
Knowing what every one knew of Basil Fitz-
herbert's attachment in the past, guessing, as he
could not help guessing, that it had been kindled
afresh by compassion after Tremayne's misfortune, he felt that he was treading on delicate
ground, and was afraid to admire, whilst he
could not condemn. "I pity her from the
bottom of my heart."

"Do you? I think she is more to be envied
than pitied."

"Why envied?" he asked in surprise.

"Because every man worships the ground
that she treads on." Her colour rose with her
vexation, as she thought of her own high-

minded, honourable husband added involuntarily
to Flora's long train of admirers.

Egerton smiled. "And *you* envy her for
that, when, if carpets were to be worn out with
worship, you would tread on bare boards for the
rest of your life!"

"Captain Egerton, compliments are odious
when you happen to be cross."

"People are never cross in society. They
leave their tempers behind them in charge of
their maids. The waltz is ended; we must
have our other turn later on. Don't let Lady
Flutterly's grandee put it out of your head," as
he saw his hostess approaching, followed by the
tall form of the Austrian *attaché*.

CHAPTER VI.

LIFTING A CURTAIN.

LATER in the evening, Lord Ravenhill was lounging against the door of the conservatory, which opened out of the back drawing-room, with a somewhat clouded face. Lost in thought, he failed to perceive the admiring glances which were thrown at him by two or three partnerless maidens, who would fain have seen his handsome head turn in their direction. Life seemed to him at this moment especially unsatisfactory, and he was in no mood for uttering soft nothings into expectant ears. He was a man who never deceived himself. He saw there was danger in constant meetings with Flora Trevellyan—he saw it most reluctantly, and with a certain sense of humiliation; but, having seen it and recognized it, he was honourably bent on avoiding them for the future. With the whole strength of his will, he was resolved to stifle his revivified passion and rise superior to it. It had once overmastered him and altered the course of his life, but never again should it have power to move him either to the right hand or the left. He no longer walked alone; there was a wife by his side, who would follow him step by step along the calm level line of content, or over the precipice of regret. He had to be careful for her sake, as well as his own; and yet his position was one of great difficulty, for he must see Lady Trevellyan rather often on her brother's account, and it would be cruelty to keep away from her, if by one word he could ease the agony of her suspense. He thought out the situation as dispassionately as he could, and soon acknowledged that, as he had chosen to stand forth as Charles Tremayne's champion, there was no way left for him but to put his own feelings out of the question and brave the danger, which he was honest enough to fear. Surely there was safety in the thought of Brenda, his pretty little wife. Where was she now? Sitting on an ottoman, with Prince Niederlohe by her side, looking down on her bouquet, with a conscious smile, to avoid his admiring glances. At a little distance stood Ronald Egerton, pulling his moustaches, with an air of discontent not habitual to his features, as he talked to a pale sweet-looking girl, with a yearning look, as if for something lost, in her large brown

eyes. Last season, she was the archest coquette
in all the world of fashion; but a change had
come over Rose Dynevor since then, and she
could not flirt with the butterflies who hovered
round her still, for thinking of the one with
broken wings in a convict's cell.

"Poor child! it is hard on her—desperately
hard;" and Basil turned away with a com-
passionte sigh, and walked with slow steps up
to the corner in which Lady Trevellyan was
seated. She was surrounded, as usual, by a
number of friends; but they moved aside to let
him pass, as a privileged person, into the magic
circle.

"Will you allow me to take you downstairs
to have an ice?" he asked, with a grave bow—
all the graver, perhaps, because he detected on
the faces of those around a slight smile and a
look of being, so to speak, in the secret.

"Willingly; the heat is overpowering." She
rose with a smile, and put her hand within his
arm. The staircase was so crowded that they
took refuge in a curtained alcove on the landing,
between the two flights.

"What news?" she said breathlessly, after
one glance round to see that the crimson velvet
couch on the opposite side of the wall was empty.
Again her love for her brother predominated
over every other feeling, and Lord Ravenhill saw

it, and was glad. It helped to make his task of self-control less difficult.

In a low, earnest voice, he told her all that he had done, and all that he hoped to do, and she listened with eyes fixed on his face and parted lips.

"And what does Mr. Goodeve say?"

"He gives very little hope; but I think he might be more encouraging to you. He seems to be prejudiced against me."

"Not likely. I will tell him that you are the kindest, best of friends." Her eyes shone.

"He looks at me as if he suspected me of some sinister design; but it doesn't matter so long as he does his best for Charlie. Are you going down to see him?"

She turned away. "I must not go. Philip has forbidden it."

Not a word of complaint, but none the less Basil felt for her acutely.

"Would it be any comfort to you, if I went instead?" he said, after a pause.

"Oh, if you only would!" and her voice trembled with suppressed eagerness.

"Anything on earth to serve you," rose to his lips; but he only answered calmly, "I will see if I can manage it, in the course of another week."

"Oh, thank you a thousand times! If you

only knew what a constant nightmare it is to me! To think that he may be actually wasting away, and I not know it! He might be at death's door, and I should not hear of it till too late." The tears were in her voice, and she controlled herself with an effort.

"No, no; I wrote to the governor, who is a great friend of Ward's, to ask him to keep his eye on him. He would be sure to let me know if there was anything wrong."

Feeling that she must not stay there any longer, she rose from the sofa. "How good you are!" she said, fervently. "May God reward you for your kindness to that poor boy in this world, as well as the next!" And in the fulness of her gratitude, she held out her hand. He took it, as a man must take what a woman offers, unless he be a churl; and as he felt it in his grasp, his head bent slowly, till his lips nearly touched it. The kiss was not given, for his will was strong to overcome his weakness; but at that instant the curtain was pulled aside, and dropped as hastily, though too late, by Ronald Egerton.

"You see, Lady Ravenhill," he said hurriedly, "there is plenty of time for another dance;" and he led her away, not wishing to make capital out of his friend's fault, only saying whatever came first on the spur of the moment.

Brenda did not answer; but she let him waltz with her again and yet again, scarcely conscious of what she did or said, whilst the scene in the alcove seemed to dance before her eyes. What had her husband meant by the ridiculous farce of the afternoon, except to blind her eyes to what was coming? He knew they were going to meet Flora Trevellyan, therefore she was to array herself in her best, in order to do credit to his taste; therefore he was anxious to make all things straight between them before they parted. Men were all alike—all faithless, and scheming, and ungrateful; and she had been only a poor deluded fool to think her Basil superior to the rest!

With these thoughts in her mind, she was inwardly indifferent to the opinion of others, but outwardly anxious to please. She made Bertram Fitz-herbert perfectly happy by a flower from her bouquet. She smiled on Prince Niederlohe, and promised to go to the Austrian fête at the Botanical Gardens, whenever it might chance to come off. She delighted Sir Philip Trevellyan, who thought her attractions superior to those of Mrs. Muncaster, because she had pretty eyes and knew how to use them, as well as to talk nonsense with her rosebud mouth; and as to Ronald Egerton, he was completely enslaved.

Sir Philip was aware of the long *tête-à-tête* in

the alcove, and thought it rather amusing to
flirt with Raven's wife, in the mean while. To
do him justice, in spite of certain jealous twinges,
he was perfectly convinced that his brother-in-
law was the principal subject of the conversation.

"And when did you arrive from Rome?"
inquired Brenda, as she tried to arrange the
flowers in her bouquet, which had been rather
deranged by Bertie's theft.

"Only two days ago, or you may be sure
you would have seen me before;" and he leant
forward with a smile.

"I can't be sure of it, as we were perfect
strangers."

"Strangers only in name—I speak for myself.
Far off as Rome is from London, we were not
quite out of your world, nor you out of mine."

"If Trevellyan were out of the world, I
wonder what would become of him," said Ronald,
in an exaggerated drawl.

"Depends upon whom I had with me," said
the Baronet, promptly. "I could fancy exile
tolerable on some conditions."

"Ah, conditions that would never be fulfilled.
I could fancy myself happy in a balloon—with
the right person."

"I couldn't;" and Brenda laughed softly.
"The coming down would prey on my mind

to such an extent, that I should never know a moment's peace."

"The dread of never coming down would be worse," suggested Sir Philip. "A trial of constancy that might turn the most ardent love into hate."

"In a man, perhaps," said Brenda, thinking of her husband. "Men are always changing."

"Never so inconstant as women. You shake your head, Lady Ravenhill; but I can prove it to you in half a dozen words. When we hover like butterflies from flower to flower, we are constant to woman in general, though not to one woman in particular. Our hearts are too large, our affections too vast, to be concentrated in a limited space; but a woman, when disappointed in the one man of her choice, goes back to spinsterhood, and is inconstant to the whole of his sex. Am I not right?"

"Of course not. Captain Egerton, say something to refute it."

"It must be a marvel of beauty, to be claimed by the whole of our sex," he answered, with a smile; "and unless the claim has been made, there would be no ground for the charge of inconstancy."

"Absurd, my dear fellow. I was affirming a general principle—it is not to be dissected like an anatomical study."

"But, Sir Philip, you gave us one instance, and Captain Egerton only made the most of it;" and Brenda looked up archly.

"If you are going to take his part against me, Lady Ravenhill, I shall think it time to look for my wife;" and he stood up, as he spoke.

"Very well, Sir Philip; and when you have found her, amuse her with an account of your new theories." Involuntarily her lip curled with a sudden remembrance.

"I keep them for my friends"—with a bow. "My wife would not appreciate them;" and with that he went off.

"A curious fellow! What do you think of him?" said Ronald, dropping into the place Sir Philip had just vacated.

"I think he is delightful; so agreeable, and so amusing."

"All women rave about him; but I never could see why."

"Perhaps because he seems to appreciate our sex more than his own."

"That is a failing common to most of us; but you never rave about me."

She looked up with a smile, and their eyes met. Of course he had spoken in jest; but there was a look of unusual gravity in his face.

"If I did, I should rather surprise you."

"You would; and I shouldn't care for it."

"I wonder where Basil is; I am sure it is time to go."

"Shall I go and fetch him?" said Fitz-herbert, ever eager in her service.

"Oh, do, please; but don't disturb him, if he is engaged;" and her face clouded as he hurried away.

"But I can tell you what would please me;" and Ronald went on, as if there had been no interruption. "If you would only say simply——"

She rose hastily, feeling that she had been rather imprudent already, and he was obliged to stand up at the same time. "I will *say* nothing. Friendship is won by deeds, not words."

"Deeds!" he said, with sudden bitterness, as he saw Lord Ravenhill coming towards them. "What is there to be done nowadays? If you would only drown, and let me save you; if your house would obligingly catch fire——"

"Hush! I was nearly drowned once; and now I wish to Heaven, that Basil had never saved me!" Without another word, she turned away and took her husband's arm, bade good-bye to Lady Flutterly, and left the room.

Dumb with amazement, Captain Egerton stood rooted to the spot.

Sir Philip, meanwhile, with a smile on his lips and a frown in his heart—if the expression may be allowed—had sought his wife in the

alcove, and found her, not with her old friend
and former lover, Lord Ravenhill, but with Miss
Dynevor, a harmless, though somewhat agitated
companion. He exchanged his intended acid
greeting for an urbane smile; and escorted the
young lady back to her chaperone with his usual
courtesy, put Lady Trevellyan into the brougham,
and, after a moment's hesitation, took his place
beside her.

So Lady Flutterly's ball came to an end; but
the consequences, like the wide-spreading roots
of the cedar, spread far and deep in the lives of
some of her guests. The hostess was perfectly
content, because the Prince vowed that he had
enjoyed himself so much that she positively must
give another before the end of the season.

CHAPTER VII.

ONLY A SUMMER SHOWER.

DARK ominous clouds hung over the usually cheerful town of Bedford, as Captain Balfour walked homewards from the barracks to the small habitation where he had lodged his bride. It was a typical little nest for a pair of lovers. On the outskirts of the town, almost in the village of Kempstone, with roses and honeysuckles growing over the porch, and hanging down in clusters over the bow windows on either side of the doorway. A tall elm-tree stood on the right, between the angle of the hedge and a tiny stream; and under its grateful shade, Balfour was wont to lie on a rug at his wife's feet, with his pipe in his mouth, and his eyes fixed adoringly on her tranquil face. But to-day Mrs. Balfour was not to be seen. He walked into the drawing-room, threw his shell-cap down on the table beside her open work-basket, unbuckled his sword, flung it on the sofa, and with his hands in his pockets,

walked back to the door. He whistled loudly,
but there was no answer. With a frown, he
betook himself to the kitchen. Benson, the
cook, informed him that "missus" was out shopping, but had left word that she would be back by
half-past four, so she was getting the tea ready.
"Half-past four! It is twenty to five now!"
and he went back to his post at the door.

A pelting shower began; the roses swayed
to and fro as their leaves were scattered on the
ground; the iron scraper filled with water, the
small round beds became so many puddles. If
he had been alone, he would probably have
let the drawing and dining rooms be inundated;
but as Kate was coming home, he went in and
shut the windows, lest she should find the rooms
damp. The path was rapidly becoming a
stream, the road a river. If she came back in
this, she would be drenched to the skin; but of
course she would have the sense to take a cab.
After a while he became intolerably restless. To
stand at the door any longer was impossible; he
would go down the road to look for her. He
stooped to turn up the hem of his trousers, and
when he recovered his perpendicular, lo! Kate
was there, struggling with the latch of the gate.
Bareheaded he rushed out into the rain, threw
open the gate, and almost carried her in.

"Kate! how *could* you?" he exclaimed in

fierce remonstrance, as he gazed in dismay at her small draggled figure, from which tiny rivulets were spreading through the narrow hall.

She laughed merrily at the fierceness of his expression. "How could I help it, rather!"

"You ought to have helped it," he said, all the more angrily because of the anxiety he had suffered on her account. "You ought not to have thought of stirring without a cab."

"But what if a cab were as much out of reach, as a four-in-hand? I was already some way on my road home when the rain began," she said, struggling to divest herself of her moist gloves. "I stood up for ever so long under a small tree, and the only vehicle that passed me was a perambulator pushed along by a nursery-maid, with her skirt over her head. I couldn't very well get into that, could I?"

"No, but I had rather——"

"What?" as he stopped.

"I don't know, but I would have given anything for this not to happen. Mary! Benson! come and see after your mistress; can't you guess that she's half drowned!" he shouted angrily.

The maid and the cook bustled out of the kitchen and took possession of Kate, who looked laughingly back at her husband as they hurried her upstairs.

"You had better have some brandy and

water," he called out. "Where are the keys?"

"I wouldn't have it for the world! The keys are in my pocket, and there they will remain."

He was still fretting and fuming, when she came downstairs in a simple evening dress of white cashmere, with dark red ribbons. All the curl had come out of her hair, and she looked rather meek and washed-out, as she pulled a low chair towards the tea-table, and prepared to sit down on it.

"Come here," he said authoritatively, pointing to the sofa; and she obeyed.

He drew her to him with a tenderness that was almost ferocious, and kissed her lips with a long passionate kiss that took her breath away. Always in his love for her there was a certain fierceness that gave it an imperious charm, and made her gentle heart thrill with terror and delight. "Promise that you will never do it again," he insisted, unreasonably.

"What, never be caught in the rain! How could I?" and she laughed merrily as she tried to draw herself away, but failed.

"It might be the death of you."

"Why should it kill me, when hundreds get wet, without so much as a cold in the head as a consequence?"

"Because you are infinitely more precious."

"Ah, you say so to-day, because you haven't had time to be bored;" and her small fingers pulled the whisker nearest her face. "Will you say the same a year hence?"

"I shall say it all my life, and you know it."

"You waited for me so long, that I began to be afraid you would think me dear at the price!" If she had known what the price was, the word would have blistered her lips.

A curious expression came over Balfour's face; but he said emphatically, "Whatever the price, I am *glad* I paid it. Yes," he continued, as if in answer to his outraged conscience, "I would do it, if it had to be done again and again."

"You talk rather grandly about a little patience;" and she looked amused.

"Patience?" he said, slowly. "There is nothing that eats into your heart like hope deferred. Those years that I waited with the constant fear before my eyes that I should lose you, were like a hell upon earth. No wonder that they made a different man of me. It was enough to turn the veriest saint into a devil; but no matter"—his voice changed. "My queen, my treasure! I have got you at last!" And he clasped her again in his arms, in the triumph of possession.

"I don't know what has happened to you to-night, Angus," she said, after a few minutes, when he let her go reluctantly to pour out the tea. "You seem so wild and excited."

He laughed; a rare occurrence with him, for it was often remarked by his brother officers that Balfour never laughed, and his smile was too sardonic to be an evidence of hilarity.

"What would you say, Kate, if I exchanged from this dull old regiment down here into the 3rd Bengal Light Infantry?" He saw that she was startled, by the way in which she paused with the sugar-tongs poised between her fingers. "Would you like to go to India?"

"Anywhere with you," she said simply; but there was a slight look of dismay in her pretty eyes.

"Anywhere? To be frozen into a block of ice at the North Pole; to be fried like a sala-mander in the South?"

"If you were frozen, I should like to be frozen too; if you were fried, I should like to be fried with you."

"If I were tried"—his voice sank low—"would you want to stand beside me in the dock?"

"Yes; and if you were hanged, we would climb the gallows together. There, are you satisfied?"

"Yes I believe you, for I would do the same

by you. Are you cold, child? I thought you
shivered."

"I have a creepy feeling down my backbone.
I shall be warmer after a cup of tea."

He rang the bell.

"What do you want?"

"A fire."

"Oh, but it's absurd. You will find the
room so hot, and then go off to play billiards
with Captain Whittaker."

"Whittaker be hanged!" and he scowled,
as if the thought of him were unpleasant.

Mary came in, and was told to light the fire.
Whilst the wood was sputtering, Kate knelt
down before it and held out her hands.

"Let me warm them for you. Why, child,
they are like ice!"

"I know they are. Don't you like Captain
Whittaker now? I thought he was a friend of
yours."

"I have no friends, and acquaintances come
and go like the rain. See, the evening is going
to be fine;" and he looked towards the window,
as if to change the subject.

"You had one friend, I know, for you introduced me to him. What has become of Mr.
Tremayne?" She looked up into his face with
innocent eyes. His expression hardened—that
was the only apparent change.

"He was tried for forgery not long ago, convicted, and sent to Dartmoor."

"How *dreadful!* But was he really guilty?"

He did not like lying to his wife. "He was *found* guilty."

"Poor fellow! I dare say it was a sudden temptation. And to think it has ruined his life! What a grief it must have been to you! You used to call him your only friend;" and her eyes were full of sympathy.

"It is an unpleasant subject," he said harshly, "and you need not harp on it. Give us a song."

"I am afraid I am rather hoarse." She moved slowly towards the piano, wondering that he did not come to open it for her as usual.

He stayed by the fire, although he certainly was not cold. Kate's words had struck home. Spoken by the lips he loved, they had power to reach his heart as no others could. As he buried his face in his hands, the whole scene of the trial rose before his eyes. Again he saw Charlie Tremayne standing in the dock, listening with blanched cheeks, as he bore witness against him. Was he to be cursed with this nightmare all his life? He threw back his head impatiently, got up, stood for some time on the hearthrug, frowning as he always frowned when in deep thought, and then walked slowly to his wife's side. "Kate, you are hoarse as a raven. Come and talk."

"My throat feels like a nutmeg-grater. I wondered when you were going to notice it."

He shut the piano with a bang, as she rose from the music-stool. "You have caught cold. I knew you would."

"And if I have, it is nothing very dreadful. I had a cough for three months last winter, but I got over it."

"But you may try that sort of thing once too often. I think you had better go to bed."

"Not I. The idea of leaving you to dine alone!"

"I am going out for a walk, as soon as I have changed my things," he said, with a glance at his soldierly habiliments.

"Then I am coming with you. It is quite fine now."

"You will do nothing of the sort."

"I shall. You can't do without me."

"I know that, but—— "

"'But me no buts.' I am coming."

"You have got on your evening dress," he said, irresolutely.

"It is no thinner than the one I wore this afternoon."

"Mind you put on a thick pair of boots."

"Regular clodhoppers;" and she laughed,

as, having gained her point, she hurried up-stairs.

"What a fool I am!" he muttered to himself. "But I can't do without her for a minute."

CHAPTER VIII.

" RAVEN'S WIFE."

"RONALD, I am going to make you furious,"
said Cuthbert Egerton, as he threw himself
down on his uncompromising sofa, after a hard
day's work amongst the squalor and misery of
his parish.

"I defy you. You never could manage it in
your life," replied the Rifleman, with a careless
smile, as he knocked the ashes off his cigar.

"But I am going to succeed to-day "—with
a sigh.

"What's up? If you think I have been
going a little too fast, I tell you the complaint
is chronic, and not to be cured by any amount
of sermons."

"It is not that exactly."

"Well, don't beat about the bush; out
with it."

"If I were you, I would not be so much
with—the Ravenhills."

"Pshaw! I thought it was something fresh. You've said that a hundred times before. Of course you wouldn't; but then you and I are rather different."

"I don't see why, in such a matter as this."

"Don't you? Your standard is as high as the sky, and mine as low as the mud; so we look at things from a different level."

Cuthbert frowned slightly, as if pained by his mocking tone. "I thought all men of honour had tolerably the same standard."

"There is no question of honour here," said Ronald, hotly. "Neither yours, nor mine, nor Raven's. You don't understand," he said more gently. "And no one *will* understand, except myself."

"I understood sufficiently to make me seriously uneasy yesterday afternoon."

"Ah, because you are a dear, old, unsophisticated thing, with old-fashioned notions, such as suit an anchorite like yourself, but would be highly inconvenient in modern society. 'Live and let live,' is the motto of the day, and so long as I do harm to no one but myself, I think you might let me alone."

"But are you sure of that?"

"Quite sure; certain as I am of death some day or other.

"You may be mistaken. But anyhow, do

you think it is nothing to me to see you pre-
paring a sorrow for yourself?" and his eyes
glistened with more than fraternal affection.

Ronald looked dreamily up at the ceiling.
"If the pleasure is sufficient to counterbalance
the pain——"

"But how can you tell that? In most
cases, the cost is never counted till the end."

"So be it."

"But you don't consider how wicked it is
to play with your conscience in this manner!"

"Wicked, is it?" and he smiled softly.
"It is very pleasant."

"Ronald, you can't be my brother, to talk
of sin like that!"—Cuthbert raised himself,
with sudden energy—" or else you are changed
beyond belief."

"Sin is a harsh term for a harmless amusement. I hope you are not going to grow hard
and bigoted, like the rest."

"I don't wish to be hard and bigoted, God
knows; but when I see a thing is wrong, I call
it by its own name—*sin.*"

"But you only see it is wrong, because you
spy at it through the green spectacles of suspicion. Look at it from my point of view, and
you will see that I am amusing myself in a
harmless sort of manner; and there is no reason
to call 'Wolf!' when nothing more dangerous

than a well-known, respectable sheep is in view.
Cuthbert, old boy, you have relieved your mind,
but I tell you frankly that your sermon has had
no more effect upon me than a drop of water on
a cabbage-leaf." He got up, threw away his
cigar, put his hands in his pockets, and looked
down on his brother with the imperturbable
smile of conscious innocence.

"Of course I knew that you meant no harm,
but you are doing it with your eyes shut;" and
he sighed.

"No, my eyes are open."

"Then you have the less excuse."

"I don't want any;" and he threw back his
head.

There was a pause. Cuthbert was the only
person on earth from whom Ronald would have
borne a word on this subject; and it gave him a
sense of uneasiness, mixed with vexation, to find
how seriously his brother looked on the matter
of his frequent visits to Grosvenor Place. He
liked to stand well in his eyes, so he made
another effort.

"Just put yourself in my place for a moment,
and imagine yourself knocking about town as I
do, with lots of friends, it is true, but only one
house at which you are always welcome. The
husband says, 'Come as often as ever you like;'
the wife never seems to find you a bore. Wouldn't

you go there week after week, dropping in
whenever the fancy took you, till it became
the one place where you could feel yourself at
home ? "

" No; I should be afraid of wearing out my
welcome."

" But the welcome never wears out. I know,
if you stayed away, you would be a fool for your
pains," he said, with heat.

" I am a fool, so my mother says."

" No, you are not; but I should have to be
a conceited idiot if I stayed away, for fear "—he
stammered, and his cheeks flushed—" of up-
setting any one else's peace of mind."

" Then be a conceited idiot for once in your
life."

" I can't "—with a laugh. "One look at
Raven's handsome phiz, and my own attractions
dwindle to nothing. I am only dangerous to
young things of seventeen, to whom a man's a
man, especially if he knows how to waltz."

" Humility is a new virtue in Captain Egerton," said Cuthbert, with a smile, as he lay on
his back with his hands clasped behind his head,
and his pale, intellectual face upturned to the
flies on the ceiling.

" I don't know what has come to me," said
Ronald, frankly; " but I am wonderfully humble
of late. I shall soon be meeker than any mouse.

Ta-ta, old fellow. Take care of yourself. Your cough hasn't gone."

"No; but it is getting better with the warmer weather."

"When the season is over, I shall carry you off to the south of France."

Cuthbert shook his head vehemently. "I must be dying before I desert my people."

"Thank you. I am not going to wait till then. You shall come with me, whether you will or no. Do you think your life is to be thrown away for the sake of a parcel of beggars?"

"That is just like you, Ro. You bother your head about me, but you won't take one bit of thought or care about yourself. I couldn't sleep last night for thinking of you"—and coughing, he might have added, with truth, as he moved his legs preparatory to rising.

"Don't disturb yourself. I can let myself out." With a nod, Ronald walked to the door, then came back. "Look here, Cuthbert, this is the last word I shall ever speak on this subject. If I go on as I have begun, it is because I know that whatever happens, I shall suffer *alone*. If I had the smallest doubt on the subject, I tell you, on my honour, that I would leave off at once."

Without another word, he left the room; and

Cuthbert knew that whatever might happen in the future, his tongue was tied.

There was nothing for him to do but to wait and hope—and pray, as Flora had prayed for her brother, that he might be kept from the evil to come.

    *   *   *   *   *

A day or two after this, Brenda ordered the brougham at eleven o'clock, and, arrayed in the simplest garment she possessed, which, after all, had nothing particularly puritanic in its character, started on an errand of charity. She was about to visit Mary Weston, a poor sick girl in Cuthbert Egerton's parish, who was dying in slow consumption; and she had planned the expedition with the greatest care. First of all, she must have the sedate brougham instead of the more frivolous-looking Victoria; she must put on her dowdiest bonnet and dress, in order to suit the character of a district visitor; then she must start at an early hour, because it was right to make a great effort in a good cause, and good people always got up early, as if bed were a wicked place to be in, in the morning, but a haven of rest at night.

Lord Ravenhill, to whom she imparted her intentions, smiled benignly, and said there could be no harm in anything that was suggested by Cuthbert Egerton, but he should strongly

object to her visiting those dirty slums too
often.

"It will be such a happiness to me, if I can
feel that I am doing some good in life," she
answered, with a sigh of unrest.

"So long as you do your duty at home and
in society," he said gravely, "you are doing
good to me and to others."

"Very little, I am afraid. You and they
would do just as well without me."

"I should be sorry to try."

"Much better, in fact, I dare say."

"From what point of view, may I ask?" and
he looked up from his paper, with a smile of
amusement.

"From every point of view," she said with
decision, as she slowly buttoned her gloves.

"Indeed, please explain."

"I am not good at explanations. If I were
out of the way——"-

"In a coffin, a prison, or a lunatic asylum?
Pray be more accurate."

"My coffin, of course. You could have a
wife who would be clever enough to understand
your speeches, and discuss all the political
questions of the day with you, when you came
home."

"Thank you. A regular man in petticoats,
the most objectionable creature under the sun.

I have enough of politics when I am out : for
goodness' sake, let me have something more
refreshing at home."

"Dear me, I thought that was just what you
would like."

"A gratuitous assumption, considering I
chose *you*, and politics are scarcely your forte."

"You might have chosen in haste, and
repented at leisure," she said significantly, and
then hurried out of the room before he could
answer.

He threw down his paper, and followed her
to the carriage. Shutting the door, he put his
head through the open window. "When I
repent, I will let you know."

"No, you wouldn't; you would die first."

He shook his head. "Where to?"

"Covent Garden, and after that to 18,
Maria Lane."

He waved his hand; she leant forward with
a wistful smile, fondly admiring his straight, tall
figure, with its manly chest and broad shoulders,
and the dark aristocratic face at the top. If
she could only fancy that he cared for her, how
happy she might be yet; but he had married
her out of pity, and that she could never forget!

Mrs. Torrington's tongue had much to answer
for. By a few careless words, uttered in a
moment of annoyance, she had endangered the

happiness of her brother, and of her brother's wife. If it had not been for her, Brenda's jealousy of Flora Trevellyan would soon have vanished before every fresh evidence of Basil's affection for herself. But she had taken from her the one firm standpoint on which her love could rest, by implying that she had been selected for a wife, not of free choice, but simply out of a feeling of honour and compassion.

"How d'ye do, Lady Ravenhill?" said Ronald Egerton's cheerful voice, as he took off his hat with a sweeping bow, and the carriage stopped at the entrance of Covent Garden. "You are out early this morning."

"Not such an effort for me as for you; so what brings you here at this hour, Captain Egerton?" and she looked up at him inquiringly, as he handed her out.

"My duty to my neighbour. I wanted to get a few odds and ends for a sick *protégée* of my brother's," he said, without the ghost of a smile, "and your advice will be invaluable."

"Perhaps you are aware that I come for the same purpose?"

"A strange coincidence, which proves that there must be some unsuspected sympathy between us. Do you think a bunch of those lilies would do her any good?"

"Yes, I should think so; the æsthetes would

be sure to recommend them as a cure.—John,
keep close; I shall want you to carry some
parcels;" and she turned to the footman, who
touched his hat and followed in her wake.

"I thought I was to be your footman on
occasions like this," said Ronald, with an air of
vexation.

"You will have parcels enough to carry on
your own account; and besides," she added
gravely, "I like to be independent, sometimes, of
amateur help."

He bit his lip. "Then I will carry my
services elsewhere."

"Do. You shall go your way, and I will
go mine."

He raised his hat, and turned away in a huff.
On opposite sides of the centre avenue they
performed their different purchases, laying in a
stock of fruit and flowers as if Mary Weston
were going to set up a stall. There was no
other lady to whom he could attach himself,
so the Rifleman walked up and down in sullen
solitude, buying this and that, with no care
and thought as to the selection; it was certainly
charity robbed of its sweetness.

Brenda, on the contrary, rather enjoying the
situation, flitted here and there, attracted by a
bunch of grapes one minute, and a nosegay of
sweet monthly roses the next. When she had

nearly exhausted her purse, she made her way to the carriage, followed by John, laden up to the chin. With one foot poised on the step, she paused to look round. Ronald Egerton was standing close by with a huge bunch of lilies, another of wallflower, a third of white roses, a basket of blood-oranges, a second of forced strawberries, and a third whose contents were shrouded in paper. He was staring intently at a plant of straggling ivy, and pretended not to know she was there.

"Captain Egerton"—he turned round—"if you happen to be going to Maria Lane, I shall be most happy to convey your parcels."

"Deeply grateful, but I would not trouble you for the world"—very stiffly, and with eyes still fixed on the ivy.

"Just as you like; there is plenty of room;" and she took her seat.

He hesitated; she smiled; and he yielded at once.

John respectfully disburthened him of his load, the carriage drove off, and he instantly hailed a hansom, jumped into it, and telling the man of a short cut, reached Maria Lane before the brougham came in sight. Brenda could not help laughing, when she saw him standing on the doorstep.

"What was the good of my carrying your

parcels, if you were going to have a hansom?"
she inquired, as he assisted her to alight on the
remarkably dirty pavement.

"I came after you as quickly as I could,"
he answered with dignity, "because I did not
think it right for you to be going about alone,
in a neighbourhood like this.—Is Mary Weston
at home?"

The frowsy-looking woman who had opened
the door gazed at the couple before her with
dazed eyes. "Never had she seen the like o'
them afore," as she told her "mate" afterwards.

"Is it my girl Polly you be askin' arter?"
she said doubtfully.

"Yes," said Brenda, gently. "We have
brought a few things which we thought might
please her. And I want to know if she would
like to see me."

"Ah, Lady Ravenhill! I thought I recognized your voice;" and Cuthbert Egerton
hurried down a crazy sort of staircase, something between a ladder and a broken pair of
steps. He came forward with a cordial smile,
which vanished directly he caught sight of his
brother. "Ronald, you here!" he exclaimed,
in tones of strongest disapprobation.

"Now that I see you in safe hands, I will
wish you good morning, Lady Ravenhill;" and,

taking no notice of his brother, unless he was included in a most ceremonious bow, Ronald walked off.

"Your parcels?" said Brenda, hastily.

He looked over his shoulder with a smile. "I leave them to your tender mercies."

CHAPTER IX.

"GOLD AND ALLOY."

"Too many good things for one house," said Cuthbert; with a shake of his head, as the footman began to empty the carriage of its contents. Besides the fruits and flowers from Covent Garden, there was a basket of pudding, arrowroot, etc., from Grosvenor Place, and the tiny passage seemed as if it could scarcely contain all the things. "Would you object to my begging a few for some other sick people in the parish?"

"Not at all; but half of them are from your brother," Brenda answered, with a blush.

"Ronald is kind, but scarcely judicious. Will you kindly select those you wish to present to Mary Weston, and I will carry them upstairs."

His manner was cold and reserved, which Brenda was inclined to resent, as she felt she deserved some thanks for her exertions. Moved by a sense of justice to the absent, she chose

Captain Egerton's white lilies and blood-oranges, her own grapes, and the pudding, etc., in the basket.

"Are these all from you?"

"No. Those are from your brother."

"Be kind enough to put his on one side. Charity is too holy to——" The rest of the sentence was lost. "Thank you. You shall present them yourself; but I will carry them for you. This is the way."

He preceded her up the rickety stairs, and Brenda followed, feeling, she scarcely knew why, like a child in disgrace. But at the sight of the poverty-stricken room, which looked poor, and mean, and dirty, in spite of Mrs. Weston's hasty tidying during the colloquy in the passage; the wasted face of the invalid, drawn with pain, and pinched for want of food; the wretched bed, with a worn-out shawl for a counterpane; and the broken panes in the window, stuffed up with mouldy paper—all other feelings were swallowed up in infinite compassion, and she stood by the bedside with tears in her eyes, and a lump in her throat.

"Why did you not tell me of this before, that I might help?" she said reproachfully.

"I never tell, unless I am asked."

"It was not kind of you, for her sake as well as mine."

"I do not wish to thrust the needs of my parish down everybody's throat. Those who have kind hearts are sure to find their way here sooner or later. But I will leave you for a few minutes, as I have to read to the man next door, and I dare say you would rather be alone."

He was right. Directly he had left, Brenda felt more at her ease. The girl's dim eyes brightened as she raised the bunch of roses to her lips. "God's flowers," she murmured. "I haven't seen 'em for two year or more. They be sweet, to be sure. They were gathered with the dew on 'em, sure*ly*."

"Are you fond of flowers?"

"They was my trade. I was up afore the dawn to get 'em, as soon as the primroses came after the snow. No matter how dark the mornin', or cold and cuttin', too. It gave me the shivers sometimes, with the nor'-easter blowin' into an empty stomach; but I liked the flowers, I did, though the gettin' of 'em, and the sellin' of 'em, in rain or shine, gave me this cough and will bring me to my grave."

"I hope not. When you are well and strong, you shan't go out to pick them; I will send them to you from my place in the country," said Brenda, encouragingly. "See, I have brought you something to make you better;" and she displayed the contents of her basket.

The girl's eyes rested on these eagerly, but
a fit of coughing prevented her from answering.
When it was over she lay back exhausted, and
her thoughts wandered. "The payson says
there 'ull be no nor'-easter up there, but the
sun 'ull allers shine, and the flowers bloom.
I'm so tired o' waitin'. And feyther, he's main
angry, when he isn't drunk; and mother scolds;
and the little uns cry, 'cos they want a bit o'
bread; but we shall bite and come ag'in up
there—and I'm weary for wantin' to go." Her
eyes closed, the hectic colour faded from her
cheeks, and with the roses still clasped in her
thin fingers, she lay as if dead.

Lady Ravenhill watched her in awestruck
silence. How rich in blessing seemed her own
life in comparison with the wretched existence
of those who were always in want, and sometimes had sickness added to their bitter needs!
She pictured herself lying ill in her luxurious
home, with every comfort and alleviation that
money could bring. What a contrast it presented to this!

Humbled at the thought of her own in-
gratitude, she crept from the room with an
empty basket and a full heart; and, after a short
conversation with the mother, into whose hands
she pressed her last half-sovereign, she descended the stairs with great caution, and found

Cuthbert Egerton waiting for her at the door, with Ronald's fading lilies lying at his feet.

"I did not expect to see you again," she said, in surprise.

"On second thoughts it occurred to me that it might alarm you to be alone in a neighbourhood like this," he said gravely, as he stepped into the street.

"It was the same kind thought which brought your brother. Is it right to let your people suffer"—with a glance at the rejected offerings —"because you happen to be angry with him?"

"Is it right to let them profit from charity offered like this?" and he touched the basket of oranges with his foot.

"I don't see any harm in it. If his be wrong, so is mine." She looked up at him in eager justification, but with burning cheeks. "We both came to Covent Garden by different ways, but with the same motive. And when he met me on this doorstep, he gave the same reason as you did just now. I thought you were always right in everything you did or said; but I can't understand you to-day."

"You can't understand, and I can't explain. But perhaps you are right," he said humbly. "I preach to others, and my own practice is often in fault." He stooped to pick up the flowers. "They are very sweet, and will gladden

the heart of Betsy Jones; and the oranges will
be delicious to a fevered throat. Believe me,
Lady Ravenhill, if I am prone to judge my
brother too harshly, it is only because he is
dearer to me than any one else, and affection
is apt to be critical."

"I know it. He talks about you as if the
love weren't all on your side," she answered,
with a cordial smile, pleased at having been
successful in his cause. "But what have you
done about the improvements? Are all your
people to be turned out?"

"Not all, thanks to your husband's good
offices. We are to have the new street; and,
in spite of vested interests, the Home Office, or
the Board of Works—I really forget which—
have consented to the erection of two rows of
houses, to be let at moderate rents, in which
those who have a business connection to keep
up will be able to find a lodging. The rest will
have to be scattered," he said, with a sigh.

"But you don't go with them."

"No; I stay behind with those that are left.
But I must not keep you."

"Then good-bye. Spare us an hour or two
whenever you can; and please tell them to
drive to Lady Grenville's."

The carriage drove off, followed by many
dirty little boys, whose radical instincts im-

pelled them to hoot, because it belonged to a swell; and Cuthbert was left on the pavement, looking doubtfully at his burden.

"Gold and alloy," he muttered. "Where will you find a motive that is not mixed? Is it for me to judge?" And, with that, he carried the lilies to Betsy Jones, and the fruit to Charlie Paine, whose broken leg confined him to a filthy bed in a loathsome alley. Surely every possible compensation was needed to reconcile him to his fate; and the oranges were a powerful argument in the favour of Providence.

CHAPTER X.

IS SHE A SHREW?

LONG ago the Ravenhills and Trevellyans had exchanged calls, just at the right moment of the afternoon for finding everybody out; but they had met in every friend's house, except each other's, and, consequently, the acquaintance would have been in a fair way to merge into something warmer, if Brenda had not persistently declined to respond to Flora's advances. A multitude of engagements had prevented each from accepting the other's invitation, till Sir Philip, annoyed at a second or third refusal, told his wife to drive to Grosvenor Place, and tell the Ravenhills to fix their own day. This she did, all the more readily because she was longing to hear some news of her brother. She thought of him by day, dreamt of him by night; but not a line was allowed to pass from her to him—from him to her. It was weary work, waiting for a day that never came, and her heart grew very heavy as the summer advanced.

Her husband adhered to his resolution not to
stir a finger towards the clearing of Charlie's
name, as Ravenhill had chosen to stand forward
as his champion. He never mentioned the
subject to his wife ; but it chafed him to know
that she was depending on his former rival for
all the odds and ends of information, which were
the solace of her life. Restrained by an absurd
feeling of pride, he would not go to Basil and
say, "This is my business, and not yours ; " and
yet he was disagreeably conscious that the world
within a world, which knows the secret affairs
of its affiliated members, wondered why he let
another man do the work which was essentially
his own, and thereby lay a claim to the warm
gratitude of his wife. The gratitude of a lovely
woman is a reward for which some men will
take no little trouble; and there were many
who, to win a smile from Flora Trevellyan,
puzzled their brains in her brother's cause.

The Master of Strathrowan, with his quiet
air of aristocratic indolence, was really one of
the most active on Tremayne's side. He did
good service by eliciting a confidence from the
gatekeeper, who had overheard the conversation
which took place between Charlie and Balfour,
under the archway into Downing Street, on the
day of the fog. Under great pressure from the
Master, he undertook to bring forward this valu-

H

able piece of evidence when it was called for.
Godfrey Vivian, a devoted admirer of all pretty
women, besides Mrs. de Vaudeville, haunted
most of the hairdressers' shops in London, in
the endeavour to identify the man who changed
the notes, and who possibly might have bought
his redundant red whiskers for the purpose of
disguise. Having been led astray by many
false scents, he found that he might have spared
himself the trouble; for Lord Ravenhill had
discovered the wig-maker who had sold a pair
of red whiskers to a black-haired man, early in
January. He had taken him in a four-wheeler
to St. Pancras' Church, on the day of Miss
Ward's wedding, and Bryant, the wig-maker in
question, had pointed out the bridegroom as the
purchaser. He knew him in a moment by the
white lock at the top of his head, which had
attracted his attention in the first instance when
the whiskers were tried on—under the excuse
of private theatricals—and which was plainly
visible as Balfour stood in his place, in the front
of the whole congregation, before the altar. It
was a strange caprice of the fate which pursued
him to cause another link in the chain of
evidence to be forged against him, at the
moment that he was uttering his marriage
vows. In every blessing he was doomed to find
a curse!

Encouraged by his success, Lord Ravenhill went to Jermyn Street to interrogate Mrs. Lloyd. He had an inward conviction that her evidence was open to suspicion, partly on account of the copious tears she had shed, principally because it was contradicted by Mary Ann, who was not likely to have an unworthy motive for the contradiction; but on arriving at her door, he was told that Mrs. Lloyd had gone into the country, in failing health, and had left the house in her sister's hands.

"When is she likely to return?"

"Pretty sure to be 'ome, missus says, by the end of the month," answered the maid.

"Is your name Mary Ann?" inquired Lord Ravenhill, with a smile.

"No, sir; Jemima Priggins."

He slipped half a crown into her hand, and went home to find Lady Trevellyan's carriage at the door. Letting himself in with his latch-key, he hurried upstairs to the drawing-room, where Flora was sitting alone, with a photograph-book on her knee.

"Where's Brenda?" he said, looking quickly round the room, as he shook hands.

"Coming directly; but she is engaged with her dressmaker, and I have begged her not to hurry. Have you any news?"—the usual question.

"Yes; good news." He closed the door, and, taking a chair beside her, proceeded to tell all that he had just gathered from the Master of Strathrowan.

Flora's eyes glowed and her cheeks flushed. "This is news indeed, for it proves that he was innocent from the very first. Thank God!" and she clasped her hands, unable to say more at the moment.

"Don't be too sanguine; the disappointment would be so fearful."

"But we can't be disappointed now."

"Yes, we can, excuse me. First, we have to prove the motive for his silence to make the story credible; and, secondly, there is the charge of complicity, which it will be almost impossible to refute."

"What *can* be his motive?" She looked up with bewildered speculation in her eyes.

"Heaven knows! I am going down to-morrow."

"You are!"—there was a catch in her breath. "I would give anything on earth to go with you!"

"How do you do, Lady Trevellyan?" and Brenda walked into the room, with an expression on her pale face which it would be hard to define.

The door being ajar in the back drawing-

room, she had come in unperceived, and just in
time to overhear Lady Trevellyan's last remark.
No wonder that her manner was cold and resent-
ful, even when she tendered her apologies for
the delay in her appearance.

The conversation turned into indifferent
channels; the various events of the season were
discussed, with interest, although the minds of
the two women and the one man, who formed
the trio, were bent on something far more en-
grossing than the topics which employed their
tongues. Lord Ravenhill was fully aware of his
wife's resentment, but at a loss to account for
it; unless she were absurd enough to object to
his entertaining a lady visitor in his own house
during her involuntary absence, which would
certainly be childish and ridiculous. It made
him uneasy, and deprived him of all enjoyment
in the society of Flora Trevellyan. With a
man's dislike of a scene, he almost wished she
would go, and yet dreaded the *mauvais quart
d'heure*, which might ensue for him on her
departure. What had come to Brenda to make
her so unreasonable of late ?

"Have you taken tickets for the Austrian
fête?" she asked, not because she wished to
know, but simply for the sake of something to
say.

"No, not yet. To tell the truth," said

Flora, with a smile, "I don't think I quite approve of it, in spite of Prince Niederlohe's warm recommendations."

"Niederlohe left Brenda no peace until she had promised to go; but I should not be surprised if she changed her mind at the last minute."

"I shall do nothing of the kind. I have promised to be there, and I mean to keep my word."

"Of course the object is good," said Flora, with her usual tact. "Nothing could be more pitiable than the position of the poor creatures who have been turned out of their homes by the earthquake. M. de Zinsky nearly made me cry with an account of their sufferings; he was so terribly pathetic."

"Victor knows how to work on other people's emotions, because he feels everything so desperately himself. He is a splendid character, ruined by his own perverted opinions, and capable of the noblest devotion, but always in a wrong cause."

"Not, surely, when he spoke so eloquently in defence of the Jews," Brenda suggested, not for love of De Zinsky, whom she scarcely knew, but from a strong inclination to disagree with everything that was said.

"No; for once he was on the right side.

But in his craze for anything and everybody that is proscribed and, as he thinks, oppressed, he links himself with Socialists of the worst description. He is the kindest-hearted fellow alive; but whilst he would contemn with horror the vivisection of a rabbit for the advancement of science, he is hand and glove with the Nihilists, who are actually, if not professedly, a breed of assassins."

"I remember how he talked about them to me at Rome. I longed for a man to support my side, for I am afraid I generally left him the best of the argument."

"Scarcely likely;" and Lord Ravenhill smiled, as he pictured the probable scene between them. "Women have no logic, it is true; but they have a way of proving their point without it."

"There is no logic like the logic of facts," said his wife, sententiously; "and there are so many to go upon in an argument against the Nihilists, that I should have thought you would have closed his mouth at once."

"Not so easy, Lady Ravenhill, when a stream of eloquence is flowing;" and Flora, with a smile, rose from her seat. "But if you will promise to start the topic with M. de Zinsky at the Austrian fête, I will come on purpose to listen to you."

"Thank you; if *you* failed, I should not have the slightest chance of success." The courtesy of the speech was spoilt by the bitterness of her tone, and Flora could not help wondering why there was no possibility of friendship between herself and Lord Ravenhill's wife, if she were ready to forget the past, and Brenda did not know of it.

"You might succeed in this line, and Lady Trevellyan in another," said Basil, stooping to conciliation. "Try your powers on De Zinsky, and leave the verdict to us."

The "us" grated on her ears. "No; I will rely on something else than my politics when I wish to make a sensation," she said, with a slight toss of her head; "and I will try my poor little powers on a man who has not been already subjugated by Lady Trevellyan's charms."

"My charms, dear Lady Ravenhill, if not utterly mythical, are certainly things of the past;" and Flora smiled, with the wistful smile that lent a peculiar grace to her beauty and a flat contradiction to her words. "But you have not told me yet which day it will be safe to fix for our little affair, in order to make sure of your coming."

After some discussion, a date was settled

somewhere about the beginning of the next month, and Lady Trevellyan departed, with the inward conviction that Lord Ravenhill had married a shrew.

CHAPTER XI.

GUINEVERE.

FROM this day the breach between Brenda and her husband widened perceptibly; it was evident in every small detail of their life. She was deeply conscious of it, and even deplored it with bitter tears; whilst by look, and word, and deed, she did her best to increase it. Lord Ravenhill watched her silently, taking no one into his confidence, as was only right and natural, and yet longing for some one to tell him the motive of his wife's behaviour. It continued to be a mystery to him, puzzle over it as he might night and day. Sometimes he would look appealingly at Lady Grenville; but she had not the courage to answer anything but a question in words, feeling that to interfere between husband and wife was in general only to add a third party to the strife. The heart of man is a strange anomaly. There are some, indeed, which beat with the regulation tick of a fifty-pound repeater; whilst others go slowly when the regulator ought naturally to be turned to "fast," and gallop when it points to "slow."

It was thus with Basil. When first married to a pretty wife, whose love for himself almost amounted to the folly of adoration, his heart had remained provokingly cold; in fact, it was only after a severe struggle and with the utmost effort of his will that he could keep it in his own possession, and not give it back to one who had no right to claim it; but now that Brenda's infatuation had changed into apparent indifference, with a perversity that surprised himself, and was utterly unknown to her, his own indifference gradually developed into something warmer. Looking at her with admiring eyes, he often longed for the kisses which he had once left, like ungathered flowers, because he had not cared to take what her pretty lips would have been so glad to give; now he scarcely liked to ask for them, lest they should be refused, or, still worse, granted grudgingly. There is nothing that enhances the value of a possession so much as the possibility of loss; and it was the fear that her affection was slipping from him that made him so suddenly anxious to retain it.

He was perfectly conscious of the openly avowed devotion of his cousin, Bertram Fitzherbert; of the hardly less open admiration of

the Austrian *attaché;* of the mutual liking which
existed between his wife and Ronald Egerton.
The first was a good-hearted boy, the second
was a mere butterfly, the third was his friend.
He saw no danger, and he was too proud to
interfere.   He preferred to stand aside and
watch, outwardly cold and reserved, inwardly
consumed with the smouldering embers of resentment.   Time after time he told himself that
all her faults came from youth, thoughtlessness,
and inexperience; another year, and she would
settle down with the quiet dignity which used
to be considered the proper attribute of a married
woman.   In modern days it was less in vogue;
but he hoped to see it revived in his wife.   In
all this he did not judge her with the harshness
that Lady Grenville had prophesied; for, although
Flora Tremayne had destroyed his faith in
woman, Flora Trevellyan had reconciled him to
her sex.

One look in her face had been sufficient to
prove that faithlessness was as impossible to her
as darkness to the sun, *ergo* the rest of women
were worthy of his trust.   A weaker man than
himself would have utterly succumbed to the
irresistible charm of her beauty, doubly enhanced
as it was by the pathos of her sorrows; and
even he, with all his strength of principle, at-
tacked by the insidious temptations of memory,

as well as by the actual attractions of the present, had found it almost impossible to act and to feel up to his own rigid standard of honour.

It was hard when the victory was won, a victory which seemed for a while to rob his life of all its sweetness, to find his domestic enjoyment spoilt by the coldness and levity of his wife. He bore it without a word; but his patience was not the result of weakness; and when the necessity for speech arose, he spoke. It was through a woman's jealousy that he first learnt that society had been amusing itself at the expense of himself and Brenda.

The Trevellyans' party came off with all the *éclat* that beauty, fashion, taste, and money could give it. Every one was there who was needed for any one's else enjoyment, and eyes that had been dim with hoped deferred, sparkled with the promise of fruition. Those who had been parted by hard-hearted mammas, met by Flora's kindly management either amongst a bower of roses or behind the shade of convenient lace draperies. She had a vivid sympathy for unhappy lovers, and "detrimentals" who were accustomed to the cold shoulder and an outside place in their homes, received a warm welcome from Lady Trevellyan to the innermost circle of honour, and voted her house an elysium.

It was a paradise for those who loved "not

wisely," from a financial point of view, but so
infinitely well; for prudence was never a great
ally of Flora's, and when she once sacrificed all
for its sake, it repaid her so badly that it was
more out of favour than ever. Therefore she
smiled on younger sons, whispered hope to the
impecunious, and turned her graceful shoulders
when she was wanted to look another way.
Parties are as plentiful in the season as swallows
in Algiers, and their repetition becomes mono-
tonous; but some notice must be taken of the
Trevellyans' "at home," because of a conversation which took place between Mrs. Muncaster
and all who chose to listen to her.

Godfrey Vivian was there, apparently fastened
by diamond cement at the side of Mrs. de Vaudeville, who threw many glances at others over her
large red face, whilst she talked to the young
attaché. The Master of Strathrowan whispered
soft nothings to his hostess whenever she had
time to heed them; and Lionel Westmacott, now
on his way from Constantinople to Washington,
told his last best story to a small audience
gathered in a corner. Peere Sylvester was
making a small amount of hay, whilst Miss
Dynevor, his temporary sun, looked out from
the clouds which usually surrounded her pale
face. And Ronald Egerton had found his way
to the sofa where Lady Ravenhill was sitting,

like a very audacious Bulbul to somebody else's
rose. Sir Philip hovered here and there, with a
special smile and a pleasant word for every pretty
woman who met his eye ; but for a certain lady
in white, with heliotrope trimmings, Mrs. Muncaster noticed, he had half a dozen words, and
at least a double proportion of tender glances.
At first Lady Trevellyan had been the object of
her dislike ; but satisfied that *she* had no wish
to exert her undoubted charms for the recapture
of her own conquests, she turned all the venom
of her hatred on Brenda, who was looking most
provokingly pretty, as she bent over the bouquet
of roses and heliotrope, which Ronald had given
her to match her dress. In spite of her eager
protestations to the contrary, Lady Ravenhill,
at war with herself and all her nobler aspirations,
had proved the truth of Lady Grenville's warning, and was no longer above the weakness of
dressing to suit another taste than her husband's. Loving him still with all the strength
of her foolish heart, she seemed madly bent on
doing everything she could to annoy him ; and
the friend who loved her like a younger sister,
watched her with pity and dismay. Would the
fit of weakness last long enough to ruin her life,
or would it end soon in a burst of tears and a
passionate cry for forgiveness ? This was a
question that Lady Grenville asked herself day

after day; but no answer came, and the evil that she dreaded rather increased than diminished.

"Dear Lady Trevellyan, do spare one minute to poor me," said Mrs. Muncaster, entreatingly, as Flora was passing with Lord Ravenhill by her side. "I have a charming project in view, and I want to ask your advice."

"If it can be of any use I am sure it is at your service;" and she stopped with a courteous smile.

"Sit down, or I shall have to shout, and I don't want to proclaim it from a housetop;" and Mrs. Muncaster moved aside her dress of gorgeous fabric.

Flora sat down with some reluctance. She disliked the "*ci-devant* beauty," and had no high idea of her discretion; but she endured her for her husband's sake, as he seemed to enjoy her conversation, as much as when he first praised it at Lady Flutterly's. Basil leant against the painted wall close by.

"And what is your project?" she asked, as she unfolded her face.

"Only this—to represent, under the guise of innocent *tableaux-vivants*, an illustrative gallery of the principal events of the season. Some of them should be so beautifully painted that the lookers-on would be obliged to clap, for fear lest some one should see the personal appli-

cation. Don't you think it would be the greatest
fun possible?" Her black eyes danced in
malicious anticipation, as she looked round to
make sure that Lord Ravenhill was within ear-
shot.

"It sounds rather dangerous. People may
do many things in private which it would be unpleasant to see depicted on a public stage."

"Of course it would be unpleasant; but that
is the spice of the pudding. It would be delicious
to see them writhing in agony, whilst struggling
in vain to keep up an amiable smile. I think it
would be the death of me!" and she laughed,
with the mischievous glee of a child of seven.
"Paris and Helen would do for that youthful
prodigy of wickedness, who ran away with a
woman who wasn't worth her railway fare.
Iphigenia might suit poor Lottie Verner, who
was certainly sacrificed on the altar of the god of
Mammon when she married old Marchmont's
money-bags."

"My ideas on the subject are very vague;
but I don't think Mammon has anything to do
with the fate of the real Iphigenia."

"Oh, never mind; she was sacrificed to
please her father, and that's quite enough to suit
my purpose. Then there's young Vivian as
Orpheus, trying in vain to win his Eurydice back
from the Hades of the stage; and, coming nearer

home "—in a loud whisper—" we have Launcelot and Guinevere before our eyes "—and she cast a significant glance at the opposite sofa—" and Arthur, feeling rather out of the hunt, poor fellow, reclining in gloomy grandeur against the wall."

"It won't do, Mrs. Muncaster," said Lord Ravenhill, stepping forward. "Brenda and I are too near the beginning of our matrimonial career to begin ' a madness of farewells ' just yet. A lady of experience, like yourself, would make a better Guinevere, and Muncaster, being so often absent, would leave more room for—— "

" Now don't, Lord Ravenhill; if you take all my nonsense *au grand sérieux*, I shall be afraid of opening my lips," she said with a pout, but her colour rose underneath her rouge.

"*Au grand sérieux*, Mrs. Muncaster; how could I ? " and he constrained his lips and eyes to laugh, as he looked down into her piquant face.

"I don't know "—she shrugged her shoulders with a smile of happy innocence. "But if you *had* been Arthur," she added slowly, "Tennyson would have had to make his Guinevere mad."

"I always thought she was," said Flora, drily.

" You mean to say that she would never have taken me ? " and Lord Ravenhill raised his eye-

brows. Secretly chafing, he seemed unusually
urbane; but he hated the pretty little coquette
with a fierce hatred that surprised himself.

" No, Lord Ravenhill "—with an expressive
glance; "but having taken, she would not have
given Launcelot so much as the tip of a finger."

" *You* can say so—a sworn butterfly warranted
to roam, to hover, and distract, so long as men
have eyes, and wings have the power to
flutter ! "

" Wings must flutter if no resting-place is to
be found," she said pathetically.

" Won't Muncaster's broad back be sufficient
for the purpose ? "

" Muncaster ? "—in infinite contempt. " He
would give me the finest horse in his stable,
and think I was the happiest woman in the
world."

" A good horse is not to be despised," said
Flora, rising. "Quicksilver is one of the greatest
blessings of my life."

" But you haven't given me a word of
advice."

" No; because you don't need it. If your
proposition had been serious, you would have
been in the position of that mythical person who
lived in a glass house, and began to throw
stones." With a glance of laughing reproof, she
moved away.

The Master of Strathrowan came up to Basil, and drew him on one side. " The proof you wanted is found," he said in a low voice, " and here is the man who can tell you all about it; " and he touched Lionel Westmacott on the arm.

CHAPTER XII.

NO FOLLOWERS ALLOWED.

"Don't go away just yet," said Lord Ravenhill, as he led the way into the library in the small hours of the morning.

"It is so late," objected Brenda, with a smothered yawn, "and Philips will be waiting."

"Let her wait;" and he closed the door behind her.

His manner was stern, his face clouded, and his tone so cold that it made her shiver. She leant against the table, her heart beating fast. He suppressed all sign of emotion, but his face was deadly pale, and his voice somewhat hoarse as he began again. "For several months I have allowed you to do exactly as you liked, and given you the fullest liberty as to all your actions. You can scarcely complain, I think, of any want of patience on my part?" He waited for her to speak.

"No; you have gone your way, and I have

gone mine," she said slowly, thinking how sweet it would have been if the divided paths had been but one road.

"Yes ; because it was your wish that it should be so ; and for that reason only."

She shook her head.

"Yes, Brenda," he insisted. "The wish was yours, not mine. Finding that you did not appreciate my society, I did not care to press it on you. Remember, I am not reproaching you for this ; but I do think you might have been a little more careful of your dignity as well as mine."

She raised her head, with burning cheeks.

"I have seen what was going on, of course; but I did not wish to interfere, so long as I could hope that your own discretion would induce you to stop it."

"Basil, what do you mean? " she asked breathlessly, with a scared look in her eyes.

"Surely you must guess. It is patent to every one, as I found to-night."

"Do you mean to say that any one dares to say that I am *not* discreet? " Her eyes flashed fire.

"I am sorry to say they do."

"Basil ! "

The word rang out like a cry of pain. In an instant she was Brenda Havergel again, justifying herself indignantly against the prophesy of foolish, light behaviour after marriage. Her head drooped in sudden contrition. Lady Grenville had known her better than she knew herself.

"Who said so?" she asked, after a pause.

"That odious little woman, Mrs. Muncaster; at least, she implied it by coupling your name in an offensive manner with Ronald Egerton's."

"Captain Egerton! Didn't you shut her up?" The forcible school-boyish expression slipped out unawares.

"No; my blood was boiling, you may be sure; but I had to be civil in order to disarm her."

"Why, who cares what she does or thinks? If she had ventured to say one word against you, I would have thrown it back with contempt in her face, no matter who was listening!"

He looked down on the ground, resting his head on his hand. "I couldn't," he said gently.

"Why not?"

"*Because I felt that she had something to go upon.*"

"*You?*"—with a gasp, and a sudden whitening of her lips.

He frowned, more with pain than anger. "Yes, Brenda, I felt it. You have been foolish and imprudent—nothing more ; but of course society will talk, if you let Egerton dangle about you every day of your life."

"And Bertie, too, and Prince Niederlohe; pray don't let all the blame fall on Captain Egerton," she said bitterly, her anger rising as she remembered how the friendship of the latter had been thrust upon her, whether she would or no.

"Why did you let them ? "

"Because I saw other women doing the same thing."

"Is that any excuse ? "

"Certainly. If I see the immaculate Lady Trevellyan, with half the Foreign Office at her feet, and you yourself"—her bosom heaved— " always at her beck and call—— "

"Brenda, you forget yourself," said Lord Ravenhill, sternly.

"No, I don't. I remember myself, and all that I have suffered but too well. *She* may do anything ; whilst I am to blame for everything, whether it is your fault or mine."

"That is absurd. How could it be my fault ? "

"It *is* yours, and yours alone. You asked us to be friends, and then, when I have grown to "—he watched her with dilated eyes—"to like him "—she looked him straight in the face

—"to like him very, very much, you coolly ask me—that is to say, I suppose you mean that—to give him up. I can't do that—he amuses me more than any one else; and I shall be horribly dull if he never drops in on wet afternoons, or when there is nothing going on."

" It is dangerous to turn a full-grown man of flesh and blood into a plaything."

" Not when the position suits him as well as me." She buried her face in her bouquet, and thought how sorry the donor would be to see how quickly the heliotrope had faded.

Lord Ravenhill studied her as if she had been a puzzle. He could see by her manner that there was no danger for *her ;* but looking at her as she stood before him, with the light from the chandelier falling full on her sunny-brown hair, and soft fair neck, as she bent over her flowers, in all the glories of her jewel-studded ball-dress, he thought that there must be a risk for his friend, and he sighed.

" What do you want me to do ? Not to forbid him the house ? " she added quickly, as he hesitated.

" No; only to let there be some limit to his visits. No man should be allowed to drop in whenever he likes."

" It was yourself who proposed it."

" Did I·? Then I was to blame in the first

instance."   Still anxious to spare his wife as
much as possible, he suggested that if she found
it difficult to manage it, he might give a hint to
Egerton.

"Not for the world!" she exclaimed, with
burning cheeks.   "I should die if he thought
that anything had been said about it."

"Perhaps you are right.   In this case, certainly, least said, soonest mended."

"And Bertie, is he to be banished, too?   The
house will be very lively."

"No; he is only a boy, and as my near
relation he can be useful as an escort."

Her lip curled.   "And the Prince?"

"Surely you can keep a man like that at a
distance?" he said, with some irritation.

"Certainly.   I can turn two cold shoulders on
him instead of one; and he will care about as
much as I shall.   But I must warn you as to
Captain Egerton, that I may seem to disobey
you when I don't mean to.   It must be done
very gradually, for if he suspected anything, I
should never be able to look him in the face
again.

"Of course you will use your own discretion"
—a quality which she was supposed to have lost.

"Having had my orders, I should like to go
to bed "—with a weary yawn—" or it will soon
be time for breakfast."

He went to the door, and opened it without a word.

She passed out with a slight bend of her head, as if he had been a stranger.

And all the way upstairs she said to herself, her fit of penitence gone like last winter's snow, "*He* may follow Flora Trevellyan about like a dog, but Ronald Egerton's frank friendship is to be taken from his wife! Oh, the injustice of man!"

CHAPTER XIII.

"HOW LONG?"

FOR the next few days she was really unhappy.
Her life seemed to be more difficult with every
week that passed. It was galling to her pride
to come back from a party, or a drive in the
Row, where she had done her best, at the cost
of her own pleasure, to avoid a friendly chat as
of yore with Captain Egerton, and find a letter,
in her husband's handwriting, lying on the hall
table, directed to Lady Trevèllyan. She might
have guessed that he wrote more often in order
that he might not be obliged to seek an interview; but jealousy is the direct enemy of common sense, which always retires when the other
comes on the field, so she was not able to
soothe herself with this consoling thought.
Lord Ravenhill had told her frankly, in the
first instance, that he meant to use his utmost
energies for the clearing of Tremayne's name;
but knowing, as she thought she knew, that

his championship, which ought naturally to have devolved upon Sir Philip, was only undertaken for Lady Trevellyan's sake, any reference to the unhappy prisoner was sufficient to rouse her anger. Therefore the subject was never mentioned between them; and, in consequence of her unreasonableness, she was free to torture herself with all sorts of wrong fancies whenever she saw her husband engaged in earnest conversation or frequent correspondence with Flora.

She was completely in the dark as to the inquiries he had set on foot, and had no idea that he was seriously in hopes of proving the convict's innocence. If it had not been for her unfortunate jealousy, she would have sympathized heartily in her husband's exertions, and been moved to the utmost compassion by Charlie's misfortunes. Instead of sharing in all his alternate hopes and fears, she held coldly aloof, refusing to ask for the confidence which he was too proud to offer. In the miseries of this world, pride and jealousy are the two most powerful factors, and those twin friends had their home in the Ravenhill household.

Basil, meanwhile, was much absorbed by his pursuit after evidence. When he went into society with his wife, he saw that she was anxious to obey his injunctions, in spite of the difficulties which arose from constant contact

with the man whom she was told to avoid, so
his mind was at rest on the score of the gossip
of the world. He recognized the difficulty of
the situation, and made all due allowances
when her resolution seemed to fail. To look
at Ronald's frank face was enough to show that
it was impossible to regard him with suspicion
as a dangerous beast of prey in an innocent
woollen hide, therefore precautions might seem
tiresome and useless to Brenda, when her own
heart told her that danger there was none.

Considering his disposition, he was wonderfully patient; but his patience might not have
been so exemplary if he had not had Flora
Trevellyan's brother to occupy his mind. When
he went down to Dartmoor, according to promise,
he found Charlie Tremayne, or Number 382, as he
was called in the prison, looking so terribly wasted
and wan in his hideous garb of yellow and grey,
that he felt there was no time to be lost if he
wished to clear his name before he died. There
was a certain coldness in his manner, for which
Basil was at a loss to account; and he utterly
refused to charge him with any message to his
sister, which surprised him not a little.

It was in vain that Lord Ravenhill, as well
as he could through the gratings which separated
them in the visitor's room, enlarged upon Flora's
intense love and sympathy. Charlie immediately

shut up, like a half-opened oyster, though the
tears came into his eyes, and his cheeks grew,
if possible, paler than they were before. He
would not be comforted by any tantalizing hope
of release, and shook his poor shaven head
irritably, saying, "What good would a ticket-
of-leave be to me? Once branded, I can never
show my face to the world."

"But," urged Basil, intent upon rousing him
from his despair, which he feared might prove
fatal to his health, "I was not talking of a mere
ticket-of-leave, but of release, consequent on
acquittal. If we succeed in that, you will be
a hero, not a convict."

"I tell you that it is impossible," he said
hoarsely, with a frown of excessive pain; and
Lord Ravenhill forbore to press him further.

The letters—the letters kept ringing in poor
Charlie's dazed mind, but how could he ask
Basil after them? Impossible! He looked at
him wistfully, longing to know the truth, and
the look was returned with interest, for Ravenhill would have given half his fortune to know
the secret of his strange silence as to the actual
forger of the cheque. Nothing was to be done
on either side. The lips of one were sealed by
want of knowledge, of the other by honour.

When he was back in his cell, Charlie turned
his face to the single pane of glass which formed

his window. The sun was slowly setting over
the distant hills. Hope, wounded on earth, had
fled with eager wings to heaven.

"How long?" he murmured, with the wild,
weary, longing of the captive for the land where
all are free. "O God! how much longer till
I die?"

*   *   *   *   *

Lord Ravenhill returned to town with a heavy
heart. A sudden fear had come over him lest
success, if it came at all, would come too late.
He thought of Flora's agonizing disappointment
if her brother died with the soil of a felon's
shame upon his name, and he pressed on his
inquiries with feverish impatience. Lionel
Westmacott turned up at the right moment to
prove that the ten pounds were a loan given
on a sudden emergency; for he met Charlie
Tremayne, after he had parted from Balfour, by
the cloak-room at Victoria Station, when he was
on his way to join Lord Ravenhill on the platform, and he told him that he had just been
obliged to borrow some money from a friend,
as he found that he had left all his cash in the
pockets of his other trousers. Moreover, Mr.
Westmacott, on coming out, noticed Captain
Balfour, whom he knew by sight, in the act of
getting into a cab. The collar of his ulster was
turned up, and his hat drawn down over his

eyes, but he could swear to him nevertheless.
This was a most important piece of evidence,
and the hopes of Charlie's supporters went up
with a bound. Mr. Goodeve condescended to
go down to Bedford to see if he could make
anything out of Captain Whittaker and his little
bill; whilst Lord Ravenhill made another but
fruitless attempt in Jermyn Street. Mrs. Lloyd,
however, was expected to return before the
middle of the next day, so he promised to pay
her a visit late that afternoon; but on reaching
his club, he found a telegram, which had just
arrived, from the governor of Dartmoor, to say
that if he wished to see convict 382 alive, he
must come at once.

He sprang into a hansom, and drove at once
to the Trevellyans. They were dining somewhere in the country, but neither the maid nor
the butler knew in which direction. He wrote
a letter, to be delivered into Lady Trevellyan's
hands directly she returned, and then drove to
Bryanstone Square. He left Lady Jemima
wringing her hands in the greatest distress, as
if Charlie had been the apple of her eye; and
then hurried to Paddington Station, whence he
sent a telegram to Brenda.

"An urgent call to Dartmoor. Afraid I may
not be back in time to take you to-morrow. Do
not be uneasy, if I am detained."

It was absolutely necessary that some one should be present at Tremayne's death-bed, if only for the sake of the chance that he might be induced to disclose his fatal secret at the last; and, if Flora must be absent, it was better that the friend who had tried so much for his sake should be there than any one else.

CHAPTER XIV.

"WAS IT FOR ME?"

A DAY before the summons to Dartmoor, Flora was lying on the sofa in her private sitting-room, with a letter in her hand, when Sir Philip came in.

"Any better?"

"No. My head aches frightfully."

"I was in hopes that you were all right, for Giuseppe has just told me that the carriage is coming round."

"Yes, so it is; for I have had a note from Mr. Goodeve, requesting me to come to Lincoln's Inn at my earliest convenience, as he has a packet of letters which he is anxious to place in my hands. He says he would have written before, if he had not been ill."

"Let him wait, then. It can't be very pressing, if he didn't disturb himself from what was probably only a fit of the gout. I don't see why you should run after him when you are really bad."

"Yes; but—I have an idea." The colour rose in her cheeks, as she felt herself on the edge of a forbidden subject.

Her husband gave her a scrutinizing glance. "You generally have. Be so good as to explain."

"I think it must have something to do with some letters Charlie spoke of. They can't be mine, for I never wrote any which deserved to be kept."

He smiled, thinking of a packet which he had fondly preserved when his love was at its zenith. It was in a small drawer upstairs; perhaps he would look at it, when he had time. "If they were his, there would be no hurry."

"Oh yes, there is;" and she raised her head, as if intending to get up, only the pain was so great that she stopped to put her hand to her forehead to still its throbbings.

"Nonsense! Lie still; if any one goes, I will."

She looked up in surprise. "But that would bore you."

"Not much; and, if it does, I can support it for once in my life. Won't you have some scent, or sal volatile, to do you good?"

"I have some eau-de-Cologne." She stretched her hand after it wearily; but he stepped forward, poured a quantity on his own

handkerchief, and laid it gently across her broad
brow. Her eyes closed involuntarily, but her
lips smiled sweetly in answer to his attentions.
He looked down on her with a softening expression on his face. He had been cold to her
ever since that day in Rome, when she told him
that Lord Ravenhill was going to take the duty,
which was really her husband's duty, on his own
shoulders. But how was it possible to hold out
for ever against a woman whose beauty appealed
to him with such irresistible power? Sir Philip's
was a love which could only be won by the eye.
If Flora had been plain, she would have been
neglected to the end of the chapter. With a
slight smile of amusement at himself, he stooped
to kiss her, then quietly left the room.

As the brougham was waiting, he made use
of it, although he greatly preferred a hansom,
unless accompanied by his wife. He thought of
her with unusual tenderness on the way. Taking
her all round, as he might have discussed his
thoroughbreds, she was a splendid creature,
utterly free from vice; and her faults, if she had
any, only made her more lovable as they took
from the frigidity of perfection. He knew that
he did not deserve to have such a wife; but, if
he didn't, he was truly thankful that she had
not married the only man who did—and that
was Ravenhill. If she had been Raven's wife,

instead of the pretty little thing who now bore his name, he knew that he would have hankered after her all his life. Sir Philip, who had known the realization of most of his hopes, thought that to hanker without success would be an unenviable position, which would not suit him at all.

Thinking thus, he arrived at New Square before he expected it. After a short interview with the solicitor, who seemed disappointed at seeing him instead of his wife, and at first refused to give up the packet, he drove home, studying the letters on the way. They were not calculated to give him much pleasure, and he reached Queen Anne's Gate in a very different frame of mind to that in which he had left it.

Entering his wife's boudoir, he took up his position on the hearthrug without a word. Frowning desperately, he plunged his hands into his trouser pockets, and stared intently at the carpet.

Flora watched him anxiously. She had rarely seen him with such a clouded face before. What *could* it be ? Surely, if there were any news of Charlie, he would tell her at once.

" Have you got the letters, Philip ? " she asked softly.

He looked at her before answering with a

fixed, scrutinizing gaze, which seemed as if he would read every secret of her soul. Finding that she did not flinch, but returned his look with one of simple inquiry, he cleared his throat and spoke.

"For the second time in my life you have surprised me. First, when you flatly disobeyed me in Paris; and, secondly, to-day, when I find that your pretended perfection is only a mask slipped on for your husband's benefit, and slipped off for your friend's."

"I don't understand," she said, in utter bewilderment. "What has this to do with Mr. Goodeve and the letters? Have you got them?"

"I have. If you want to read them over again, to gloat over them, you needn't ask Ravenhill's permission. He treasured them, no doubt, when they were new, but now that he has chosen another star for his worship, it is a different matter. Prudent Benedicts usually destroy such tender relics; *he* gives them into other hands. What his object was, I cannot guess."

"But what are they?" and she raised herself up on one elbow, puzzled by his words as well as his manner.

"What are they? Oh, delicious from his point of view—perfectly intoxicating! From mine "—and he frowned darkly—" they are *shameless*. To think that you, whom I thought the purest of women, could have penned them is the greatest disappointment of my life."

"I? Philip, what *do* you mean?" She looked at him with wide-open eyes.

"Look here, Flora, you know what I mean, well enough;" and he went on with concentrated bitterness. "Perfect women, who descend from their pedestals, do a thousand times more harm than open flirts, like Lulu Muncaster. From *them* we know what to expect, and are secure from disappointment; but if we find that the absolute purity of others is soiled, if only in a word or a thought, then our faith in all virtue is destroyed, and we lose the last possibility of reverence for the rest of the sex. I loved you once, God knows! and I have always reverenced you, even in your coldness, thinking you were too near the angels to feel perfect sympathy with a man like me."

"Philip, what have I done?" She got up from the sofa and went towards him, still with the bewildered expression on her lovely face.

He stepped back, as if he did not wish to have her near him; and yet, as he acknowledged to himself, no angel from heaven could have looked more innocent. He sighed with excessive bitterness. How easy it was to see through Lord Ravenhill's game, now that he had the clue before him! These letters in Balfour's hands, delivered up at the demand of Charlie Tremayne, supplied the key to the mystery. It must be in the hope of recovering *them* that Ravenhill was striving with might and main in Charlie's cause. They were to be the reward of his devotion, and Goodeve had made a mess of the whole business, and given them up to the wrong person. If it had not been for the mere accident of a headache, he would have been hoodwinked to the last.

Flora put her hand upon his arm; he shook it off roughly. It made him sick to think of his wife's part in the affair.

"Flora!" he cried, with sudden passion, "how could you stoop so low? I would rather have seen you dead, than lived to despise you!"

"You are under a strange mistake," she said gently. "Give me the letters. If they are bad, they can't be mine."

He took them out of his pocket and handed them to her, watching her closely as she opened them rapidly one after the other, the colour mounting high in her cheeks.

"My God! to think she wrote them!" and, writhing with pain at the thought, he turned away, put his arm on the ledge of the mantel-piece, and rested his head on it.

In a minute he felt his wife's hand pulling at his coat-sleeve. "Philip," she said, between laughing and crying, "these are stupid, clumsy forgeries. You couldn't have thought I had written them? Were you only pretending, in order to frighten me?"

He raised his head quickly. "Forgeries? It is easy to say so—prove it."

"Look at me, and doubt me if you can;" and her eyes flashed, though her voice was as soft as usual. "They are too disgusting; too—what shall I say?—*effrontées*, for even such a woman as your friend Mrs. Muncaster. Only read them. I feel as if it soiled my fingers to touch them." Her lip curled with disgust, as she flung them away—somewhere, anywhere, out of her reach.

Sir Philip laid his hands upon her shoulders, and fixed his piercing eyes upon her face. "Before God and your own husband, will you swear that these letters were not written by your hand?"

"I swear it; but," she added slowly, "I think the doubt is the grossest insult that was ever offered me."

"You don't know what it was to feel it. But was I to blame? The handwriting is exactly yours; the signature is yours; and Ravenhill was the only man in the world of whom I have ever been jealous."

"You have no excuse for it, whilst I, if I chose," she said sadly, "might be jealous of half the world."

"Say, if you cared. You never *did* care, or I might have been very different."

"No; it is your nature."

"It is my nature to care for every woman who is lovely. Don't be angry with me, Flora; for are you not the loveliest of them all?" and he attempted to draw her to him, with an admiring smile.

She drew back. "Those letters—if you had liked me ever so little, you never could have thought that I had penned them."

"You are mistaken; the warmest love is the most addicted to jealousy. But if they weren't yours, whose were they?"

"Simple forgeries," she said disdainfully.

"Yes; but forgeries for what end?" His brow contracted in deep thought. "I have it!" he exclaimed excitedly, after a pause. "The blackguard! the scoundrel! Don't you see? He forged these letters; he held them over the poor fellow as a threat; he said, 'Betray me, and I'll expose your sister to shame. Hold your tongue, and I'll keep them dark;' and he held his tongue for your sake, and he went to prison and to penal servitude to save you; and I have let him lie there, poor dear boy!"

"Who did it?" said Flora, breathlessly, every scrap of colour fading from her cheeks.

"Who? Balfour, his dearest friend; the man against whom I warned him. He shall pay for it, the scoundrel! I should like to thrash him within an inch of his life before I send him to the dock; but my first duty is to Charlie. I will go to the Home Secretary at once; and to Dartmoor by the first train to-morrow morning. Don't cry, dear; your brother will be the hero of the day Noble fellow! to think how I misjudged him!"

"Oh, was it for me?"

Sobbing passionately, Flora flung herself upon his neck. For once, at least, her heart beat in complete unison with her husband's, as he strained her to his breast. There were unaccustomed tears in his own eyes as he stooped to kiss her hair, and, after a minute or two, gently unclasped her arms and placed her on the sofa.

"I must be off, or I shall not catch him before dinner." Looking back over his shoulder to meet her grateful glance, he hurried out of the room; and Flora was left alone to utter a fervent prayer to Heaven, that the hope which had just been given might not be quenched ere fruition.

"Oh, to think that he suffered it all for me!" With clasped hands and shining eyes, she sat still and pondered.

CHAPTER XV.

" YOUNG, AND SO FAIR."

"OPEN the window, Angus; I can hardly breathe," murmured the weak voice of Kate Balfour on a glorious day towards the end of June.

Captain Balfour rose from the chair by her bedside, and walked slowly to the window. It was open as wide as could be, and the sweet summer air, laden with the scent of roses and mignonette, was pouring into the room. He tried to push it further back; then leant out, with an impatient sigh. Why should his wife be ill? She was young and fairly strong, perfectly healthy till this horrid cold came on, with no signs of incipient disease on her sweet fair cheeks, where the roses came and went with every changing tide of feeling. It was just like his cursed ill luck. She was more to him, he fancied in his egotistic fashion, than other wives were to their lords and masters. Other men might work, and struggle, and fret and fume, for wives

that were hard to win; but few had sinnèd as
he had, and his sin made her all the more dear
to his heart, for we value many things in proportion to their cost; and the more we pay, the
more we prize.

"I doubt, after all, Kate, if India will suit
you," he said, looking out into the small garden,
and seeing nothing of its summer beauty.
"People ought to be strong as horses to en-
counter such a change of climate."

"Some one told me that it made strong
people weak, and weak people strong," she said
softly, as she moved her head restlessly on the
pillow.

His quick ear caught the movements, and he
returned to her side at once. "You are not
comfortable; let me move you."

"Only raise me up a little. I want more air."

"Your chest is worse?"

"My cough is better," she answered, with
affectionate evasion; "and that is a great thing.
Would you mind cutting off this troublesome
hair? It makes me so hot."

"I couldn't;" and he frowned, as if the
suggestion hurt him. He had not the heart to
cut a lock of hair off his wife's head, and yet he
could betray his friend with a tolerably calm
countenance.

"But, Angus, it destroys my comfort, and

cropped curls *à l'Olivette* are all the fashion,"
she pleaded, with a smile.

He took her pretty locks up in his hand, and
kissed them. A sunbeam shot across the bed;
and lighted its luxuriant brown masses into
waves of gold. Good heavens! to ask him to
destroy such loveliness! The idea was not to be
thought of. Kate would be the first to call out
at his barbarity when she was going to her next
party.

"My scissors are somewhere in the room."

"We will wait till you can get up and fetch
them for yourself," he said, with a smile.

"Then you will wait till it's too late;" and
she turned away, with the irritation of a helpless
invalid when refused a slight service which she
longs to be able to do for herself.

"And when it is too late to want them, you
will thank me." She did not answer. He bent
over her persuasively. "Kitty dear, you won't
look half so pretty without it."

"Never mind, if it makes me a little less
uncomfortable."

"Shall we wait till to-morrow; the weather
may have changed?"

"Yes, if you like; and when to-morrow
comes——" She stopped, exhausted.

He looked at her with an anxious frown.
"Would you like me to go for Dr. Mitford?"

A slight shake of the head.

"I wonder if she ought to have any more medicine?" He took up a bottle on a small table, and examined the label. "Every four hours; and I gave her the last at two o'clock." He poured a dose into a glass, and put it to her lips. She drank it thirstily; then presently dropped asleep. He sat by her for a long while, listening to her fitful breath. It came in stertorous gasps, every one of which threatened to disturb her rest; and his heart grew almost mad with fear as he waited. Patience is a necessary virtue in a sick-room, and patience he had none. It was impossible to him to sit calmly by Kate's side and see her suffer, although the pain of man, woman, or child had rarely, if ever, excited his compassion before. To her he could be as tender as a woman; to others he was capable of the cold cruelty of a savage. He would scarcely have shrunk from cannibalism if it had been for his own good to fatten on the flesh and blood of his fellow-creatures; and in a case of starvation by shipwreck, his comrades would have done well to give Captain Balfour a wide berth.

He went to the door softly and called Mary, the maid. She ran upstairs at once; for women-servants are generally obedient to a handsome master, and prove their æsthetic proclivities by

their appreciation of his good looks. Having
told her to remain with her mistress till his
return, he went out. He could not rest without
the doctor's opinion on Kate's state. She seemed
to him much worse since the morning. The
oppression on her chest had decidedly increased,
and her strength was less. He knew nothing of
illness, it is true, and the signs might deceive
him.

Dr. Mitford was out, but would probably be
back by eight o'clock, when Captain Balfour's
message should be given him. Obliged to be
satisfied with this, Balfour called at the barracks,
and arranged for his absence till the end of the
week, if his wife were not better by that time.
He then went home, had some dinner, and
resumed his former post. Kate was still sleepy;
but her long lashes rested on fevered cheeks,
and her lips were parched. One arm was thrown
outside the prettily embroidered quilt, and even
in sleep her fingers played restlessly with the
muslin frill.

Balfour tried to read, but the effort was
useless; the lines ran one into the other, and
made no impression on his brain. Would that
confounded doctor never come? He threw
down his paper and went to the window. It
was a perfectly cloudless evening, without a leaf
stirring. It seemed as if the sun in sinking to

rest had taken the air to its bed of glory. The earth seemed to pant, the flowers drooped, the birds were silent. Only tireless gnats hung about the roses, as if anxious to steal their last sighs, whilst their lovers, the bees, were sleeping.

To Captain Balfour nature was ever a closed book. He noticed that it was a remarkably stuffy evening, that the scent of the jessamine was unusually powerful, and with a muttered curse at the heat, turned away. As he did so, there was a sound of light wheels on the road and a dog-cart drove up to the gate. Dr. Mitford, a grey-whiskered, sensible-looking man, of an average height, got down, and Balfour went up the path to meet him.

The visit had to be a short one, for the doctor was on his way to another patient, who had sent for him in a hurry; but he looked long and steadfastly at Kate, felt her pulse, asked her a few questions, promised to send another draught, and, with a cheerful "Good evening," left the room.

Balfour followed him in silence, afraid to ask the question which hung upon his lips. Dr. Mitford stopped at the door of the dining-room, and stepped inside.

"What do you think of her?" said Balfour, hoarsely, constrained to speak because the doctor was evidently waiting to be asked.

"She is in a very serious state," he began slowly.

"Tell me the truth;" and he held the doctor's arm tight. "Is she in danger?"

"Yes, in great danger."

"But she will get better?"—with his whole heart in his eager eyes.

"She may; but, to speak honestly, I do not think it." He saw the large eyes dilate, the white face turn almost to green, and, accustomed as he was to sorrow, his heart bled.

Without a word, Balfour gathered himself together, as if after a heavy blow, and led the way into the garden. He watched the doctor depart, then returned to the house with a slow step.

He could not face his wife just yet. Boys, when stunned in a football match, were always left quiet till they came round; and he must have time to recover from the greatest blow that was ever dealt by the cruelty of fate. Time to recover! Would he ever be his own self again, able to go back to drill and the mess; to busy himself about the small details which make up the sum of life; to care if dinner were hot or cold; if a bill were paid or unpaid; if men were civil or uncivil; if things went right or wrong? He sat down on a chair, leant his elbows on the table, his face on his hands. A fierce rage was

burning in his breast, a rage against Providence,
who took his only hope from him, his one ewe
lamb. What if he *had* sinned? Kate was innocent—innocent as any child before it knew a
wish or a want that could tempt it astray. In
common justice—the justice that men dealt each
other here—the punishment should fall on *his*
head, and not hers. Take her to heaven, and
she *must* want to come back if he were left
behind. In his wild, uncontrolled passion he
had no conception of the higher, holier love,
which raises heart and soul above the level of
earthly ties and absorbs the conflicting streams
of mundane desire into one wide ocean of all
sufficient tenderness. He judged her by himself. There would be no room for him in this
world, or the next, without his wife. It seemed
as if his soul, like the wandering Jew, would
rove restlessly from sphere to sphere, always
asking for its other self; always asking, never
resting, always craving for the answering voice
that never would be heard. He *could* not live
without her. It was absurd, impossible! What
was the good of marriage, which made them one,
if death had the right to part them into two?
It was all a mockery from beginning to end.
There was no logic in the decrees of Providence. Charlie Tremayne was innocent, and a
prisoner. Angus Balfour was guilty, and went

at large. Kate had done no wrong, and she must die!

Why had he been allowed to succeed in his wretched fraud if the object for which he had forged, and stolen, and lied, was to be taken from him when he held it in his hand? The voice of the tempter was in his ears, "Curse God, and die!"

He groaned—more like the angry growl of an enraged beast than the moan of a man in sorrow. His fingers clutched his hair on either side, and he ground his teeth with the rage of baffled love in its useless strife with death. There was not a single crime known to man which he would not have been ready to commit, if the sin would have kept Kate by his side till the end of his days; there was not a virtue known to the angels which he would not have striven to attain, if the good that was in him could have formed a chain to bind her to earth. It is probable that he would have failed in the pursuit of virtue, but he was capable of any effort for the sake of the one being whom he cared for far more than himself. He felt no remorse for the wrong that he had done to Charlie Tremayne, but he dreaded the retribution, which was standing on his very threshold; and in order to avert it he was ready to own himself guilty and release Tremayne, if only death would have held its hand. With this

thought in his mind, he pushed his chair from
the table, gave a look of surprise at the darkening
room, and went upstairs. No one can tell what
it was to him to go in to his wife, knowing what
he knew !

CHAPTER XVI.

RETRIBUTION.

SHE looked up at him with eager eyes full of love's earnest longing. "Why were you away so long?"

Her voice was so low that he had to kneel down in order to hear it. "I couldn't help it." There was a change in her face, and he noticed it at once. "You don't feel so well? Is there anything I can do for you?"

"Only stay with me as long as you can;" and her fingers closed tightly over his.

His heart seemed to contract within his breast. Was it too late? Was this the greyness of death already under the lovely eyes and about the sweet, soft lips? Or was there time to undo the wrong that he had done, and appease the insatiate hunger of Fate for vengeance. A telegram to Lady Trevellyan would be all that was needed; she and her friends would do the rest. He actually started to his feet, with the inten-

tion of sending it off; but Kate looked up in
alarm, and whispered, " Don't leave me."

" Only for one minute, dear. I will be back
directly."

" No ; stay with me." And he stayed.

How the hours passed he never knew. He
knelt by the bedside, their hands clasped, their
faces close together on the pillow. The doctor
had promised to come before twelve, if possible ;
but Balfour knew that no doctor on earth could
do any good. Sentence had been given, and
Kate must go. He waited without a hope, without a prayer. A God whom he had scorned in
every action of his life would be scarcely likely
to listen to his first entreaty. Prayer would be
mockery on lips that had never prayed before.

" My dear father," murmured Kate. " Give
him my love. I should like to have seen him
once."

" To-morrow I will send."

" Tell him that I always loved him ; and let
him have my Bible."

" You may give it him yourself."

" Raise me up; I cannot breathe."

He lifted her head gently, and placed his
arm behind it to support it. " Is there *nothing* I
can do for you ? "

" If you would read a hymn or a prayer," she
said hesitatingly.

"Oh, not now. Talk to me—think of me while you can." Selfish even at that moment, he thought more of his own love than of her salvation, as he fixed his passionate eyes on her face.

"Darling, I think of you; pray for you always. God has been so good to let me be with you a little while before He took me."

"Good?" His lip curled; but he could not utter all the evil in his breast in the face of her sweet resignation. His heart was bursting, and he laid down his head with a groan. There was a ring at the front door. Neither the cook nor housemaid had cared to go to bed, so it was promptly answered, and Mary came upstairs with a letter in her hand. She entered the room on tiptoe, and placed it on the bed. "What do you bring it for now?" he said fiercely; and she replied in a loud whisper, "The gentleman said it was very particular, sir, and was to be given to you at once." Then she went out, with her apron up to her eyes.

"Read it; it may be from papa."

"Scarcely by private hand;" but he took it up listlessly, and opened it with some difficulty, his right arm being imprisoned behind Kate's head. Perfectly unsuspicious of its contents, he read it out :—

"If you have any reason to fear the reopening of the Drayton *v.* Tremayne trial, you had better fly at once.—From one who was once your friend."

The paper fell from his hand; the writing was Captain Whittaker's, and he recognized it without difficulty. At any other moment the news would have filled him with horror; now he viewed it with supreme indifference. What mattered it if he went to prison or the gallows? He could care for nothing if Kate were dead. Turning to her, he saw that her eyes were fixed upon him with a look of startled inquiry.

" Why should you fly ? "

" Never mind, dear; don't think of it."

" Fly ! " she murmured; " only the guilty fly. What can he mean ? "

" It is only some nonsense of Whittaker's."

" It sounds so earnest—as if—as if—there were some danger."

" If there is, I'll risk it."

" But you—tell me the truth, Angus. It isn't kind to deceive me."

" I can't, dear; let it rest."

But it seemed as if she could not rest. His manner was so strange that the oddest misgivings came into her mind. Curious fancies as to what the letter could possibly mean worried her tired brain. Surely, no one would have written it, if there had been nothing to fear.

What was it? Tremayne! where had she heard the name before? Of course he was her husband's greatest friend; and the trial—she remembered it all.

"Tell me, Angus; it frightens me," she said faintly.

And he; how could he lie to his wife on her death-bed! "I was so mad to win you, Kate, and your father was so resolved not to let me have you without a certain sum, that I would have sold my soul in order to get it. I forged a cheque; it was for you, dear. They thought it was Tremayne——" He stopped. Her eyes, still fixed upon his, seemed to force the words out of his mouth. "He went to prison—and I was able to marry."

"*Angus!*" There was a world of amazed reproach in the single word, which came as a last sigh from the lips that he loved. He bowed down his head without a word.

When he raised it, Kate's had fallen back upon his arm, her eyes were closed, and her lips parted. The shock had killed her!

Charlie Tremayne was avenged!

For an instant, Balfour's brain reeled. He drew her cold cheek to his, and pressed a rain of passionate kisses on the lips which could not give them back. He called her by more endearing names than his tongue had ever learnt to utter. He besought her to speak, if only one little word! He caught up her beautiful bright hair, and buried his face in it. To think that she had gone from him with the horror of his sin for her last thought! Was anything wanting to the measure of his woe? He threw himself across the bed, and lay there like a stone. Come shame, come death, he no longer cared. He had but one vulnerable point, like the heel of Achilles, and the last shaft had struck home.

CHAPTER XVII.

HOPES AND FEARS.

"WELL, I've seen the Home Secretary;" and Sir Philip threw himself into an armchair, with an air of impatient fatigue. Flora looked up eagerly. "Nothing can be done as yet."

"Not yet? I thought he would be released to-morrow," she exclaimed, in bitter disappointment.

"To-morrow? Why, there is all the evidence to be gone through first. I asked G—— to go with me, as I know it is no use trying to interest one of the bigwigs without a friend at court; and H——, I must say, was very civil. He was up to his eyes in work, but he listened attentively, and promised to lose no time when the papers were once in his hands."

"Can't we do something this evening?" and Flora started up impulsively. "It seems dreadful to keep the poor boy there one single half-hour longer than necessary."

"These things are never done in a hurry.
H—— said something about writing to the
judge—Baron Brown, I think it was. He will
have to wait for his answer; and then, if all
goes well, there will be the pardon to get."

"A pardon? What for?"

"A pardon for having been incarcerated in
one of her Majesty's gaols by mistake. It is
the way of the law. Like a woman, it hates
to own itself in the wrong, so it gets a pardon,
which you don't want, instead of asking yours."

"What an odious shame!" cried Flora, indignantly, as she thought of Charlie—*pardoned*
for the noblest self-sacrifice that man ever made.
"I call it nothing short of an insult."

"Still, it is an insult that I shall be very glad
to get for your brother."

"Yes; anything for release!"—with a sigh
of infinite longing. "When is the trial to be?"

"There is never a second trial after conviction on a criminal charge. If the evidence is
sufficient to establish his innocence, the Queen's
'gracious pardon' is extended to the prisoner,
and he is released forthwith. But if there is a
flaw—— "

"But there shan't be."

"You mayn't see it; but the eye of a lawyer
is sharper than yours. What does Ravenhill
say?" he asked, with some reluctance.

"He is confident of success. But I think he said there was still a link wanting."

"One missing link will spoil the whole;" and he frowned. "Men who have not been trained to the sort of thing are sure to make a mess of it. He would have done much better to leave it in Goodeve's hands. By-the-bye, I thought Ward was his solicitor."

"Yes, and Captain Balfour's father-in-law. It would not have done to ask him to take up a case against his own son-in-law."

"No, of course not. As to Balfour, the cowardly brute, I feel as if I could scarcely keep my hands off him. A sound horse-whipping would do him good; but I suppose it would rouse his suspicions, and I don't want him to give us the slip. Good gracious!"—looking at his watch—"it is a quarter to eight. Let us have some dinner."

"Tell me, first," she said, laying her hand on her husband's arm to detain him, "do we go to Dartmoor to-morrow?"

"No. I find that prisoners, even in the privileged class, are only allowed one visit a quarter. Ravenhill has been there once or twice, hasn't he?"

"Once, I think, not more;" and her eyes drooped.

"I dare say, under the circumstances, I

might induce H—— to give me another order; but I feel that I must be on the spot at present. Goodeve ought to be looked up the first thing to-morrow morning, and Ravenhill. I believe the clues are in his hands, are they not?"

"Yes; he has been the most active. Oh, Philip"—and she clasped her hands upon his shoulder—"it is such a joy to me to feel that you are working with us!"

Thinking of his own late inactivity, and the reason for his want of exertion, Sir Philip reddened. "If I had known what I know now," he said slowly, "I should have been the first, instead of the last."

In pursuance of his resolution, he paid a second visit to Lincoln's Inn the next morning, and was kept by Mr. Goodeve for such a time that he did not reach Grosvenor Place till Lord Ravenhill had already started for Jermyn Street. Brenda was out, so no message could be left with her; and, thinking it would be better to write a letter from his own house, he returned to Queen Anne's Gate, where Flora was waiting for him to escort her to a dinner at Richmond.

Sir Robert and Lady Grenville were host and hostess on the occasion. M. and Madame de Biron, who had come over to London to enjoy the latter end of the season, were amongst the guests, which included a goodly number of the pleasantest people in town. The dinner was at the Star and Garter; and the guests so much enjoyed sitting out .in the delightful moonlit gardens in the cool of the evening, that they were extremely loth to tear themselves. away and face the stifling heat of the metropolis. It was close upon midnight when the Trevellyans drove up at their own door, and the butler came forward with Ravenhill's note in his hand.

Flora clasped her hands in silent agony. To die in a prison, when release was close at hand! Sir Philip's voice recalled her to herself. He looked up from Bradshaw, which he had been studying hard.

"There is no train till nine o'clock. Impossible to see H—— at that hour in the morning. I wonder if I could catch him to-night?" Turning to the butler—"Send for a cab."

"What for?" said Flora, looking puzzled.

"For an order. We cannot get in without it." Noticing how ill she looked, he added kindly, "Go to bed, dear; you will want all your strength for to-morrow."

Without a word, she turned away and went slowly upstairs, feeling as if leaden weights had been added to each foot. When Wilton had taken off her pretty shimmering dress, she threw herself down on the bed. Impossible to sleep whilst her heart was crying through the long watches of the night, "Wait for me! wait for me! Don't die till I come!" She felt as if that might satisfy her, only to see him once— to touch his hand, his lips, and tell him how she loved and blessed him for his sacrifice.

Big Ben tolled out the slowly passing quarters; and as soon as the first ray of dawn appeared, carts began to pass along Birdcage Walk, laden with fruits and vegetables for Covent Garden market. It was useless to stay in bed and listen to the growing noises of reviving life, so she crept out of it very softly, for fear of awaking her husband; and when Wilton came into the room, with a smothered yawn and a can of hot water, she was surprised to find her mistress already dressed, and sitting at the table writing a letter.

CHAPTER XVIII.

RATHER RECKLESS.

"ANYTHING the matter, Lady Ravenhill?" said Ronald Egerton, as he seated himself in a low chair close beside the sofa, in her boudoir. He had an uneasy consciousness that a coolness had arisen between them lately, and he came this afternoon with every intention of dispelling it.

After all that had passed between herself and her husband, Brenda expected to feel a certain restraint at the first meeting; but anger is an irresistible distraction, and shyness was driven away by indignation.

"Everything, Captain Egerton. I never was so cross in my life;" and she tried to pout, instead of smiling.

"Indeed? You must be very bad."

"And so would you be, if you were me," she exclaimed, grammar having yielded to excitement.

"Tell me what it is, and perhaps I shall be, although I am not," he answered, with a smile.

"For weeks and weeks I have set my heart on going to this Austrian fête. I almost swore that nothing should prevent me."

"Nothing shall "—very quietly.

"Excuse me, but something has. Only five minutes ago, I had this telegram from my husband, to say that he is called away to some outlandish place, and he is afraid that he won't be able to take me."

"Then somebody else must."

"Lady Grenville is not going; and it isn't every one that I would ask."

"Every one isn't wanted. But surely your sister, Mrs. Hayward, would come to the rescue."

"Augusta? Her hair would turn grey at the thought of it. She thinks all fancy balls rather fast, and this one particularly naughty. I am always doomed to be disappointed, if I care for a thing overmuch;" and she looked ruefully down at the carpet.

"You shan't be disappointed. If I put on a grey wig, don't you think I should do for a chaperon?"

"No; you would never do for a chaperon, if your hair were as white as snow."

"Never? Is my old age to be robbed of its only solace? But, joking apart, somebody must be found, and the time is short. Let us set our brains to work at once. Your charming little sister in your romantic home on the Wandle? I am sure she would come, if you asked her."

"Of course she would; but——"

"And with Fitz-herbert and me for an escort?" he said, leaning forward, and looking with unconcealed eagerness into her face. If she really wished to give him his *congé*, she would be sure to refuse; if she meant their friendship to continue, she would accept.

Conflicting doubts and wishes bewildered Brenda's mind. Thinking of her husband's injunctions, she hesitated to disobey him so flagrantly; thinking of her many wrongs, she longed to punish him. She looked up and met Egerton's eyes. "Yes," she said, doubtfully; and the expression of his face was radiant.

He rose from his seat. "There is no time to be lost. If you will write a telegram to your sister, I will take it to St. James's Street, and hunt up Niederlohe at the same time."

"What for?"

"For a ticket. There were none to be had yesterday for love or money; and Mrs. Muncaster was tearing her hair because she could not get one."

"Then there will be no chance for Edith;" and her face fell.

"When Niederlohe knows that your coming depends upon hers, he would tear down the palings to let her in."

He went off with the telegram in the highest spirits, found the Austrian *attaché* on the steps of his own club, explained the circumstances of the case to him, and obtained the promise of a ticket without difficulty. It was perfectly true that all the tickets were exhausted, but if Lady Ravenhill wanted another, one should be printed expressly for her use; and Niederlohe smiled as he pulled the long ends of his moustaches.

The telegram caused a flutter of excitement at Jessamine Lodge. Nothing had been seen or heard of Brenda for an extraordinary period of time, and Mrs. Havergel was beginning to be anxious. Augusta Hayward had paid several visits lately to her former home, and, according to her wont, took the opportunity to throw out dark hints about her sister's conduct. Captain Egerton was described as a bold, bad man, who haunted Brenda's steps wherever she went, and would certainly end by compromising her before the end of the season. Even Mrs. Torrington was represented to have said that his conduct was *hors de règle*, and her brother must be blind and deaf to allow such things to go on. Bertie Fitz-herbert was also in disgrace for the same reason, and Prince Niederlohe's name was introduced to lend an extra flavour to the little *entremets* of gossip.

The mother sighed; Mary shook her wise

head and grieved over the temptations of the
world; but Edith indignantly scouted the idea
that Brenda could possibly be in fault, and went
up to town the first thing the next morning,
fully prepared to be her champion. She was
rather taken aback to find that, in consequence
of Lord Ravenhill's absence, they were going to
the ball under the escort of the first and second
delinquents, and that she owed her ticket to the
courtesy of the third. But how could she utter
a word of reproof when Brenda, after hugging
and kissing her with rapturous affection, led her
upstairs to see the lovely costume which Philips
and a dressmaker were concocting together
under her orders, and for Edith's own benefit?

They went for a drive in the afternoon,
chatted and laughed over gossip and shopping;
but as the day wore on, Brenda's eyes moved
restlessly from the clock to the door, and if any
one came in, in a hurry, she nearly sprang out
of her seat. If she caught Edith's eye, she
immediately began to rattle away about the
various events of the last few weeks; but sisters
are not easily deceived by such stratagems, and
Edith was convinced that something was weighing on her mind. What could it be? Perhaps,
out of mere gaiety of heart, she had gone too
far with Captain Egerton, and was thinking how
best to draw back without an open rupture; or

was it that Lord Ravenhill had disappointed her in some way, by a little less care for her comfort, and a little more neglect of her society? Various hypotheses floated through Edith's brain, whilst she pretended to be engrossed with a new piece of work; and, suddenly looking up, she made her feeble protest, hoping to find out the real state of the case.

"I suppose it is all right for a married woman to go out with two young men, but it seems rather odd to me."

"It might be odd," said Brenda, quickly, "if one of them weren't my husband's relation, and there were no other lady going with me. As it is, none but the veriest old prude could find anything to grumble at. I suppose Augusta has been talking as usual. If she can't make a grievance out of those of her own household, she invariably turns to her sister's. Of course she says I am an awful flirt."

"Nonsense, Bren."

"Oh, she does, I'm sure. And who's the man? One would think that Basil was a scarecrow, from the way every one seems to think that I like somebody else better."

"Indeed they don't; but supposing that there is any talk at all about him," she said softly, "don't you think it is a pity to go to the ball with him to-night?"

"I think it is a pity that you should, if you don't like him;" and Brenda's cheeks grew hot. "I will go alone with him and Bertie, and not mind it in the least." No name had been mentioned; but conscience told her that the indefinite "him" must apply to Ronald.

"On the contrary," said Edith, with a smile, "I have set my heart on going, and I like him very much."

"Then come and dress; we shall only be just in time;" and she led the way upstairs.

*　　*　　*　　*　　*

The two sisters looked charming, in costumes borrowed from a popular opera of the day. Brenda in white satin, embroidered in pearls, with a lace ruff, puffed sleeves, and a voluminous train. Edith in short petticoats, showing off her small feet, looked very piquante in a cream-coloured upper skirt over quilted rose satin.

CHAPTER XIX.

THE AUSTRIAN FÊTE.

If Lady Ravenhill was preoccupied and uneasy, Ronald Egerton was suffering from an unusual depression of spirits; and the onus of the conversation devolved principally on Edith and Bertie. To the former, such a festivity as the Austrian fête was an unprecedented piece of gaiety—her eyes sparkled with excitement, and her tongue went as fast as the carriage-wheels; and the latter was full of fun as any schoolboy, his cousin having lately insisted on paying his debts. Freed from the burden of care, which had been rather oppressive to his young shoulders, he was ripe for any folly; and Brenda had more than once to rebuke him laughingly for his happy impudence.

The fête was given in the Botanical Gardens, Regent's Park, kindly lent by the fellows of the Society for the sake of its charitable object. The tickets were only a guinea; but they were

sold under the strictest supervision by private
agents to friends of the members of the com-
mittee, alone; and great care had been taken to
keep the company select. The Austrian ambas-
sador interested himself particularly about the
arrangements; his charming wife superintended
the decorations of the huge marquee, with its
black and yellow flag waving beside the Royal
Standard, placed there in honour of the expected
visit of the Prince of Wales; and the whole staff
of the embassy were supposed to have worn
themselves to shadows by their exertions.

The gardens were exquisitely lighted with
lamps covered with silver network, which
glistened in the moonbeams; flowers met the
eye in every direction; flags waved overhead in
pendent steams of brilliant colour from long
ropes suspended from tree to tree; a Hungarian
band of rare excellence, hidden in a bower of
ferns and wondrous shrubs, discoursed the
sweetest strains; a continual ebb and flow of
gay costumes passed along the principal walks;
and a buzz of many tongues that never ceased
made an animated whole, bewildering to the
senses of those who were freshly arrived. Brenda
pressed nervously to Captain Egerton's side;
Edith followed close with Fitz-herbert. Amongst
all the crowd of faces not a familiar one was to
be seen; and the two sisters noticed with some-

thing like dismay that many of the ladies wore black-lace masks, whilst a large number of the men appeared in domino.

Brenda looked up into her companion's face in order to gain reassurance from a certain happy confidence which never forsook him; but he was unusually grave, and at that moment engaged in scanning the crowd with an uneasy air. Was it Mademoiselle Fridoline of the Covent Garden ballet who had just passed him by with a saucy look? He could not be sure; but the girl's glance was sufficient to show him that she did not belong to the same world as Raven's wife, and he began to wish that the carriage had not been sent away. It was, however, too late for regret, so they pressed on, and, after a good deal of patience, reached the marquee. Dancing had already begun with animation. The melancholy strains of Strauss's last waltz sighed sweetly through the tent; and there was a flutter of silks and satins, and jewels and velvets, as light feet gyrated over the white drugget, and light laughs echoed from breathless lips.

"Will you try a waltz?" said Ronald, as gravely as if he were propounding a solemn thesis in religion.

"Not yet, I think. Like a person beginning to skate, I want to feel sure of my ground.—Ah, how d'ye do, M. de Zinsky? Have you seen

anything of the Trevellyans ? '' Brenda extended
her hand with a cordial smile, and asked the
question which was most likely to interest him,
in her delight at meeting a friendly face belonging to their own set.

"No, madame!" and he raised his eyebrows
disconsolately. "There is no chance for to-
night. Miladi Trevellyan has gone to Devonshire."

"Indeed! How unkind to the Agramese!"
Her colour rose, as she thought of her husband's
sudden call to Dartmoor. Those two must be
always together; and it was convenient to have
a brother who always wanted you and your
special friend, on every emergency.

"Very unkind to them, and to all her
friends," muttered the Hungarian, evidently
like a spoilt child—he wouldn't be comforted.

"I will dance now, if you like," she said,
turning to Captain Egerton.

"*If I like!* "

After a few turns, they stopped. "I have a
fancy to-night that, although some of the people
seem rather excited, no one is really happy;"
and Brenda fanned herself languidly. "Look
at that girl over there; she looks downright
miserable."

"She is evidently dancing with the wrong
partner."

"And so might you be; for you look like a mute at a funeral."

"Perhaps I am," he interrupted with a smile; "but if so, I would rather have the wrong than the right. Let me have another turn before Niederlohe pounces on you."

Slowly, but in perfect time with each other's step, they made the circuit of the room, and stopped for a breath of air by the door, as the music ceased. Fitz-herbert and Edith passed by on their way out, and, after a few remarks on the bystanders, disappeared into the gardens.

"Lady Ravenhill, I have found you at last," said an eager voice; and before Brenda knew he was there, Prince Niederlohe bowed low over her hand. "For the last half-hour, I have been standing at the gates watching for you; and yet I must have missed you by some unlucky chance. I was afraid that Milor' Ravenhill had made his appearance at the last moment, and ruthlessly destroyed our hopes."

"You would scarcely have noticed the absence of one amongst so many," said Brenda, with a smile.

"Not when I would have sacrificed the many for the one?"

"You would have found it rather difficult to make a ball out of one solitary woman, and about five hundred men."

"I would not have made a ball, but a *tête-à-tête*."

"Then the Agramese would have suffered, and no one would have been pleased."

"Except your devoted Max "—in that delicious undertone, when everything is said in a few words.

A burst of music proclaimed the beginning of another dance, and numbers of people trooped in at the open door. Several male friends came and grouped themselves round Lady Ravenhill; but the Prince still kept his post at her side. Impatient at the interruption, and finding that private conversation was no longer possible, he suddenly informed her that both his *chef* and his *chefesse* were especially anxious to be introduced to her, and asked if he might have the honour of presenting her to Madame la Comtesse.

Brenda acceded with a gracious smile, and rose at once, anxious to rid herself of her present surroundings, and, above all, desirous of shaking off Niederlohe, whose manner added to her uneasiness. She looked round. Fitz-herbert was nowhere to be seen; Ronald was lounging against the doorway, his tall manly figure set off by the dark green uniform of the Rifle Brigade, as the light of a coronal of wax tapers shone down on his close-cropped head and the fair frank face, which some women had loved, and could never forget.

He was watching, as she crossed the room on Niederlohe's arm—watching every movement and expression as she stood amongst the group of pretty women and aristocratic-looking men, which the charming Countess K—— had gathered round her. Presently a Lancers was formed, and Brenda, after some hesitation, consented to take part in it, with Niederlohe as her partner. Ronald folded his arms, and frowned. He was feeling his position acutely. He had come to the ball as her escort, and he felt he had the right, in the absence of her husband, to take care of her through the evening. But if he did so, those cursed tongues would wag faster than ever, and he would be injuring the woman to whom he had sworn that he would never cost one moment of sorrow, be his own fate what it might. A hint from Lady Grenville had opened his eyes to the false position in which a married woman may be placed by the devotion of a friend, even if the man be nothing more than a friend to her, and his lips be sealed by every tradition of his life. Rather than compromise the pretty, innocent girl, who had crept into his heart against her will, he would spoil his own life without a thought—give up his appointment at the Horse Guards, and apply for leave to join the rest of his own brigade in India. Cuthbert would miss him, and no one else.

Some one touched the Prince on his arm. He bowed low to Brenda, and stepped aside. Bertie Fitz-herbert took his place, as he hurried away, and looked down with delight at his cousin's wife. "At last I am happy."

"Have you been taking good care of my sister?"

"Yes; most excellent. Vivian has just asked to be introduced to her, and she is dancing with him now. It wasn't very cool of me—was it?"

"Not very. I like Mr. Vivian."

Conversation could only be carried on at intervals, owing to the figures of the dance.

"I wonder if anything has gone wrong? After that mysterious whisper, Niederlohe looked quite aghast. Did you see?"

"No; I didn't look at him."

"He looks at you so much that I long to kick him," said Fitz-herbert, fiercely.

"Pray restrain yourself. If necessary, Basil will save you the trouble."

"But I have the right to do it in Basil's absence."

"Have you?"—with a smile.

"Here he is back again, confound him! Say you would rather have me."

"Can't"—as, the dance being over, she took the Prince's arm, and they both disappeared into the garden, but only on the way to the refreshment tent.

In vain he tried to persuade her to remain with him, as he poetically expressed it, "under the stars." She insisted upon being thirsty, faint, anything, rather than tarry for a sentimental *tête-à-tête* in the dusky light. Remembering her former resolution "of the two cold shoulders," she did her best to keep him at a distance; but he would not be repelled. There was an absence of restraint in his passionate glances, which roused her resentment, and yet there was nothing that she could lay hold of in his words, so long as she regarded them merely as light badinage. He had lost the respectful deference of manner which he was in the habit of assuming when talking to a star of the *haute volée*, and he laid his homage at her feet so openly, that even Countess K—— had shrugged her pretty shoulders with a gesture of amusement.

Oh, why had she ever come? She longed to be safe at home; longed to be anywhere away from this horrid man. Out of sympathy for Edith's love of dancing, and the few opportunities she had of indulging it in sleepy Inglefield, she had taken care to introduce her to a lot of partners; and now she was sorry that she had not glued her to her side. If

Edith had been there, the Prince would not
have dared to say " Not yet," when she begged
him to escort her back to the dancing tent, and,
in defiance of her request, slip into the chair
beside her.

She looked away from him across the table,
richly laden with fruits, and flowers, and dainties,
of every season.   The room was almost empty,
except for the waiters, who were gathered
together in a knot, and talking in eager whispers.
Something had evidently happened, and, turning
to her companion, she asked what it was.

"Nothing.   Only a small *contretemps*, which
need not interfere with your peace, or my happiness."

She rose determinedly.   "I am going into
the other tent, Prince.   Accompany me or not,
as you prefer."

" Cruel! " he murmured, as he gave her his
arm.

She drew up her long neck disdainfully, and
hurried to the door.   When they reached it, he
turned his steps towards the starlit gardens.

"Not there," she said hastily, and looked
round for any one in the shape of a friend to
rescue her from her present position.

Her heart was beating fast with anger and
fear, when suddenly came the welcome voice of
Ronald Egerton, as he placed himself in front

of them. Stiff and stern, he looked straight into Niederlohe's face, as he said briefly, "This is our dance, Lady Ravenhill."

It was not true; but oh! how rapturously she withdrew her hand from the Austrian's arm, and placed it in that of her faithful friend!

CHAPTER XX.

UNDER THE WILLOW.

OVERCOME by a variety of unpleasant emotions, Brenda burst into tears. Ronald hastily turned away from the crowd of loiterers in close proximity to either tent, and, leading the way down a secluded path, stopped when they reached a comfortable sofa, half hidden under the boughs of an American willow. It was a trying position for a man whose passionate sympathy must be kept to himself, when heart and honour were at variance, for the first time in his life. Brenda sobbed hysterically. From every point of view, she saw a miserable outlook for herself. A woman, taking advantage of the immunity offered by a mask, had whispered in her ear—

> "Gather ye rosebuds whilst ye may,
>   Your raven far is flying;
> The queen of flowers, as they say,
>   Is one for whom he's sighing."

The verse had not missed its aim. The queen

of flowers evidently pointed to *Flora* Trevellyan. Her own jealous heart supplied the details. She saw herself deceived by her husband, compromised by her own folly, without a single friend to whom she could turn for consolation. All would shake their heads with that hateful phrase, "I told you so!" She hated the Prince for the advantage he had taken of her position; and to Ronald Egerton, whose different conduct she appreciated most heartily, she must scarcely express her gratitude by word or look, because of a wretched woman's tongue, which had linked their names together.

"Lady Ravenhill, what is it? Tell me, for Heaven's sake."

"Nothing," she gasped, making a futile effort to regain her composure.

"Is it Niederlohe?"—with a scowl.

"No; that is——"

"If it *is*"—and he looked what he was—capable of murder.

"It is everybody and everything," she cried incoherently; "and I'm the most miserable of women!"

She bent her head down almost on her knees, and sobbed again. He was standing in front of her, looking at her with eyes full of infinite compassion. She seemed such a child in her sorrow —a child to soothe and comfort into joy. Presently he sat down, and leaning forward, rested his elbow on his knee, his head on his hand.

Two men passed along the path in front of the seat, carrying some heavy ropes and a large net over their shoulders, with something in their hands which looked more like guns than working implements. They spoke to each other in gruff whispers, and kept their eyes fixed on a clump of variegated shrubs just opposite. Evidently on the look-out for something or some one, they both started off in a hurry, when a man stepped suddenly out of the darkness beyond the reach of the silver lamps, and made a sign to them to join him. After a little subdued talking, they all disappeared. Under any other circumstances Ronald's curiosity would have been roused, and he would have jumped up and followed them, but a small brown head was raised, and a certain tear-stained face was turned to his, and he could think of nothing else.

"Can't I do anything for you?" he said hoarsely.

"No one can help me; and though all the world talk of it, I must be silent."

"You can't have heard anything to-night?" he said, in growing wonder.

She nodded.

"Then tell me;" and his voice shook with eagerness; "I ought to know. What was it?

Could it—could it have been about me?"—in a whisper, as if the leaves must not hear.

"No"—in quiet surprise. "It was a woman who said it; and she knew where to hit me hardest."

"Could it be Raven?"

"Yes; my husband"—bitterly, as if the mention of his name opened a fresh wound.

"Your husband?" he said softly; "surely he might be safe." A pause. "Tell me all; it may be better for you and him in the end. Remember, I am the friend of both."

"I know it. You have proved it a thousand times."

"Then trust me again."

"My duty as a wife forbids it."

"You have a duty to me as your friend. Don't you acknowledge it?" Bending forward, he looked pleadingly into her eyes.

Her lip trembled; she tried to look away, but his eyes seemed to chain hers. They were sad and troubled, and his face had lost its calm. "Captain Egerton," she cried impulsively, "I have no right to blame him; he loved her long ago, before he ever heard my name!"

"Then it's the old story about Lady Trevellyan," he said slowly. "I should have thought that a malicious woman would have invented something newer."

"It is no invention. What am *I*, to make him forget her—the loveliest woman in England?"

"His wife; and that is more than enough for Raven. Can you, who know him so well, doubt that? In sight, or out of sight, you may trust him, as you would yourself. Neither by a wish nor a thought, will he go beyond the straight line of duty. Made of better stuff than most of us, he is out of the reach of temptations—to which some succumb." His voice, which had been raised in earnest defence of his friend, sank mournfully to the end.

"But if a man once loves with all the strength of his nature, do you think he ever forgets?"

"But do we ever love with all the strength of our nature? I hope not; or where should we be, if our love went wrong? Some men find it hard to forget, and others feel it equally difficult to remember."

"Basil is amongst the first," she said, with a mournful smile; "and you, I fancy, must belong to the second."

"I? Of all men in the world, I am the most faithful," he exclaimed, in indignant surprise. "Have you ever seen me waver for half an evening? Have I not been your faithful friend and adviser ever since the first day of our acquaintance?"

"Ah, yes; but then friendship is so different."

" So different, that they are sometimes taken for one another," he went on, with growing bitterness; "and then the fool who has made the mistake, pays for it with the happiness of his life."

" I know it; " and she clasped her hands in an access of pain. "And isn't it enough to make me curse the day that I was born, to find that I am a burthen and a dragging tie, when I was silly enough to think I might be his joy ! "

He looked bewildered. "I was not talking of Raven."

" Yes, you were. He *has* made the mistake, and he pays for it every day of his life. He thought he could forget her, but he can't. Every week they are thrown together; he—— "

" That would make no difference to him. He has the strength of will and the strength of principle of a moral giant. Every feeling is under subjection, and he is not liable, like other men, to be blown here and there by every gust of passion. Raven is the best man I know, barring my brother."

" And you are the best of friends."

" He doesn't think so. Sometimes—lately— I think he hates me."

" Captain Egerton ! " The colour slowly

stole into her cheeks, and she rose from the seat, remembering all too vividly that her absence might be remarked.

"He has no reason to, Heaven knows. But when I am no longer here to bother him, he may think of me with some of his old kindness."

"You are not going away?" She looked up at him in dismay.

His face was white, and beneath his fair moustaches his lip trembled. "I think so."

"Oh, don't; I shall miss you so terribly;" and she put out her hand as if to stop him.

He held it in both his own. On the brink of separation, his heart was dangerously weak. He thought of Cuthbert and his timely warnings. If he had only heeded them before it was too late!

Growing nervous, she tried to withdraw her hand, as her eyes sank before the intense wistfulness of his.

"I shall never ask it again," he muttered, in hurried excuse, and raised it to his lips.

At that instant steps came round the corner; a loud rustle was heard in the bushes, every leaf and branch seemed to quiver, and with a crash of breaking stems a huge form stepped slowly and majestically on to the dewy grass, and stood before them in unmoved contemplation. Good God! it was a lion escaped from the Zoological

Gardens, and the men he had seen before were cognizant of his escape. Natural instinct made Ronald place himself in front of Brenda, who was absolutely petrified with terror, and after feeling in vain for his sword, which he had left in the ballroom, he wrenched an iron stake, which supported the branches of the willow from the ground, and held it as a lance or shield before him. With eyes fixed on the animal's glaring eyeballs, he waited with set teeth for the onset. There was a sound of hurrying feet in every direction; but he saw nothing but the great beast, who stood perfectly still, doubtful whether to advance or retreat. One bound, and they might both be dead. If he could but defend her —and die !

Men were stealing stealthily from the background with a huge net, ready to snare the lion, if possible ; others had their guns pointed to shoot him, if necessary. Every breath was held in the moment of awful suspense. Some one stepped forward unwarily, and a woman screamed. As if angered by the sound, the lion began to lash the ground with its tail. A keeper, scenting danger, lowered the muzzle of his gun. The beast bent down his huge head and gave a roar, which shook the ground ; and then, gathering himself together, rose with a sudden spring. The iron stake snapped like a ramrod, his hot breath came

upon Ronald's cheek, and without a cry, he was
flung down on the ground at the feet of the
woman he had tried to save. Shot after shot
rang in the air. The lion, who always hesitates
before seizing his prey, rolled over, before he had
time to use his claws. A man, with more courage
than the rest, rushed forward, and, snatching a
gun from the keeper next him, fired a volley at
close quarters right into the beast's mighty head.
The huge limbs quivered, the broad chest heaved,
and with a sigh of passing strength, the lion was
dead!

All had passed in the space of a minute; but
sixty seconds to those who were watching the
chances of life or death had seemed as many
hours. Having given the beast his *coup de grâce*,
Lord Ravenhill, who had just arrived in time,
caught his wife to his breast, as she was in the
act of falling, with arms pitifully outstretched to
the man lying at her feet. Ronald's head was
resting on the edge of her satin train. Niederlohe lifted it with care, and turned the white face
upward to the light.

"*Mon Dieu!* " he muttered, " the poor fellow
is dead."

Now that there was no danger, an eager crowd
gathered round, and looked with curious eyes at
the scene.

" Not dead! " said Lord Ravenhill, hoarsely.

"He *can't* be dead—only stunned." Only a few minutes before he had doubted his loyalty; now he would give his right hand to call him back to life. "Amongst all these people isn't there a single doctor?"

"Yes, sir; I am Dr. Weston, at your service," and some one came forward in the grotesque costume of the Lieutenant du Diable, and kneeling down with a professional air, he unbuttoned the dark-green uniform, and laid his hand on Ronald's heart.

Breathless silence! Every head bent forward; the light of the silver lamp streamed down on the glistening satin of Brenda's dress, as, unconscious of all that was passing, she drooped like a broken flower, supported by her husband's encircling arm—on the silver badge of the soldier's pouch-belt—on his yellow hair soaked with blood—on the upturned, deathly, whiteness of his face as he lay on the grass before her. And only those two so principally concerned were unconscious of the absorbing interest of the moment.

Dr. Weston raised his head. "There is a feeble fluttering at the heart. He lives, but for how long I can't say."

"But he was only knocked down; the lion was shot before it had time to injure him,' said Basil, eagerly.

"I think his friends have more to answer for than the beast;" and he smiled, sardonically. "There is a bullet in his shoulder; and it is the bullet which will kill him. If you are a friend of the gentleman's, sir, I advise you to have him carried home at once."

Lord Ravenhill's heart swelled as he looked down on the man who had been his friend from boyhood. Were they to part thus—without a word or a handshake? Countess K——, with the tears running down her cheeks, offered her carriage for Egerton's use. It was a landau, therefore more suitable for the purpose than the Ravenhills' brougham. Niederlohe, Vivian, and a host of others volunteered to go with him. Edith and Fitz-herbert, who had come up when all was over, and stood transfixed with horror on the edge of the crowd, were beckoned to the front.

"Here, Bertie, you go with him; I must take Brenda home. You know where Cuthbert Egerton lives; let him be fetched at once, and Dr. Martin. I will come round so soon as I have placed her in safety"—with a look at his wife. "And, Edith, keep close. You needn't be frightened, child. She isn't hurt." After a few more directions, Lord Ravenhill hurried off, being feverishly anxious to carry Brenda away from the inquisitive eyes of the crowd.

He strained her to his chest convulsively, as he threaded his way through the lamplit gardens to the gates. Only ten minutes ago, in the bitterness of his heart, as he saw her under the willow-tree with her hand raised to Ronald's lips, he had thought she was unworthy of his love; now that he had so nearly lost her, he realized for the first time what life would be without her, and, worthy or unworthy, he knew that he loved her with his whole heart. "God be thanked!" he murmured, as he stooped his head to kiss her.

"Did you speak?" said Edith, timidly.

"No," he answered shortly—like all Englishmen, anxious to hide his emotions.

CHAPTER XXI.

DARTMOOR.

It is a long journey, under the most favourable circumstances, from Waterloo to Tavistock, the nearest station to the convict prison at Prince-town; and it seemed utterly interminable to Flora Trevellyan, when every hour of delay might make it too late for her to see her brother in life. Amply provided with books and papers, she could not read a word, but sat with her hands clasped together, and her lips often moving in prayer. All through the sorrows of her past, religion had been her only support, the one comfort to which she could turn without the chance of a rebuff. Without its calming influence, her troubled brain must have given way; and she wondered how others could get through the trials of the world without its abiding stay. Captain Balfour, and such men as he, did they give one thought to the joys of heaven, when they sold their souls for the perishable things of earth? Had Charlie thought of his God, when the face of man was turned from him in scorn?

"This is Honiton, Flora?". Her husband's voice roused her from her reverie. "The tower of St. Michael's looks well from the top of the hill, doesn't it? but it must be a pull to church for the asthmatic members of the congregation."

She murmured an assent, and looked with indifferent eyes, first at the church and the Bishop of Llandaff's obelisk, and then at the tall chimneys of the iron founderies, potteries, etc., which disfigure the neighbourhood of the lace-making town.

They both got out at Exeter, and had some luncheon. After a short walk up and down the platform, they resumed their places, sighed, yawned, and consulted their watches. Would the journey ever be ended?

Sir Philip again tried to interest his wife, pointing to a fine spire at Crediton; a celebrated trout-stream a little further on; but he saw it was of no use, and presently relapsed into silence, which was not broken till the train wound slowly round a curve into the picturesque town of Tavistock. There was no time lost in getting out. Sir Philip's hand was on the handle of the door before the station was entered, and he gave an exclamation of surprise as he caught sight of a well-known figure standing on the platform.

"I thought you would come by this," said Lord Ravenhill, with a smile, as he held out his hand to Lady Trevellyan.

She looked up into his face with an eager inquiry in her eyes, which her lips refused to utter.

"Better; the sight of you will do more to revive him than anything else. Give him some hope, and I feel sure he will pull through."

"Hope!" said Sir Philip, "we can do more than that;" and in a few words he told him sufficient to show that Charlie's silence was explained, and the real culprit discovered.

"There is a fly at the door with a pair of horses, so you shall lose no time;" and Basil, after expressing his amazement, turned to Flora, with ready sympathy for her impatience.

"We are *sure* to see him?"

"Yes, sure; I have spoken to Major ——, and he expects you."

"The only thing we have to do is to send the necessary proofs in to the Home Secretary as fast as we can;" and Sir Philip followed his wife to the carriage.

"Yes; I will see about it the first thing to-morrow morning. Good-bye."

"Are you not coming with us?" they both asked in surprise.

"No. My train starts in a quarter of an

hour. I have an engagement at home, and I must not disappoint my wife; " and, after earnest thanks from one at least, he turned back into the station.

Seated in the open fly, with the pure, sweet air of the moor blowing in her face, Flora Trevellyan breathed again. She had no eye for the interesting points in the landscape, with the grand old Tors on the left, looking blue in the afternoon shadows; the leafy birchwood on the right; the Tavy swollen with last week's rain. They came back to her in after years as a picture burnt on her brain; but she saw nothing now of moor, or peak, or silver stream; only in the distance a massive pile of buildings, seated on the slopes of South Hessery Tor, guarded by walls and watch-towers, and every device that man could suggest for the safe keeping of his fellow-man.

As they drove along the broad military road which surrounds the high walls, and stopped before the granite gateway, with its noble motto, "Parcere Subjectis," on the keystone, Flora's heart sank, and with a sudden feeling as if she dared not enter for fear of what she might find within, she sat still, though Sir Philip was holding out his hand to help her to alight.

It was not the usual hour for visiting, but the order was taken into Major ——, the governor,

who came out to receive them. In consequence
of the special circumstances of the case, an
exception was made in their favour.

"And how is Tremayne?" inquired Sir Philip,
anxiously, after a few commonplaces had been
exchanged.

Major —— looked puzzled. "Ah, 382, you
mean. I remember. We have nothing but
numbers here—no names. He is a little stronger
to-day, according to the doctor's report. The
visit of his friend Lord Ravenhill seemed to do
him good; but you shall judge for yourselves."

He led them past the belt of gardens and the
parade-ground to a second gateway, which is
never left unguarded by day or night. Passing
through this, the governor pointed to a long row
of buildings, four storeys high, as the dormitories
where the prisoners were lodged at night, and
in the day, when not at work or chapel; but,
in consequence of illness, 382 had been removed
to the infirmary.

Flora walked by his side as in a dream—
the massive walls, the heavy locks, the barred
windows, the guards, and watch-towers bringing
before her mind so vividly the utter hopelessness
and helplessness of convict life that she felt
choked and oppressed, as if the heavy iron and
mortar were literally weighing on her chest.
She let her husband ask all the necessary

questions as to the cause of Charlie's illness, and his actual state, listening to the answers, it is true, but taking no part in the conversation.

It appeared that convicts, on their first arrival, if in ordinary health, and suffering from no physical infirmity, were set to work on the bogs. No. 382 took his turn at peat-cutting like the rest, and worked with a vigour that surprised his guards. The surgeon, fearing that he was overtaxing his strength, suggested that he should be set to some lighter work in the quarry; but any change of the kind is against the custom of the place, until the convict has become, by hard labour for a year and strict attention to discipline, what is called a " privileged man." 382 made no complaint, and toiled diligently through cold and heat, probably, as his sister thought with an aching heart, to drown his wretchedness in the lethargy of utter exhaustion, and win the freedom of the grave. A violent storm had raged over the moor at the beginning of the preceding week, and the gang with whom he was working came back to the prison soaked to the skin. None of the others had suffered, but 382 caught cold; inflammation of the lungs set in, and his fever was so high that Major —— thought it advisable to telegraph at once to Lord Ravenhill.

"His pulse has gone down, and there is nothing now to fear but weakness."

"But surely, with youth in his favour, he will soon recover his strength?" and Sir Philip stood aside to let his wife pass up the flight of stone steps to the infirmary.

"You must recollect that life does not seem a very desirable thing in a convict prison."

"No; I understand that. But there is every prospect of Tremayne being released before the week is up."

"In that case, hope may save his life. Tell him that he will be free, and that will do him more good than any medicine. This way, Lady Trevellyan."

In another minute, she was standing by the bedside of 382, looking down, through a mist of tears, at a close-cropped head and a haggard face, that seemed but a horrible travesty of the good-looking, bright-eyed young fellow who went by the name of Charlie Tremayne. Unmindful of the eyes that watched, she slipped down on her knees, with a little wail of pain.

"Charlie," she said timidly, as she laid her hand on the thin fingers which appeared over the edge of the coverlet.

A slow smile crept round the drooping mouth; a sudden light of recognition into the large eyes, dim with the hopelessness of months; a cavernous voice came from the pale lips—" Flora ! " That was all; and then, with a quiver of joy, the two faces met.

Major —— considerately walked away; the warder stood motionless at the end of the room; Sir Philip waited in awestruck silence, his worldly but kindly heart touched to the core.

A long silence, broken by Charlie as, with trembling fingers, he stroked his sister's lovely face. " I'm glad to have seen you once."

" Yes, dear "—with a catch in her breath like a strangled sob. " Once to-day, and again to-morrow, and then we shall be always together."

" Not yet. Philip will be wanting you ; you can't be spared."

" No ; but Philip will be with us. He is here. Don't you see him ? "

Trevellyan bent forward and extended his hand. Tears, unaccustomed to such a resting-place, were in his eyes. " God bless you," he murmured hoarsely, his heart swelling with the thought that it was love for his own wife that had brought the poor fellow to this.

" Ravenhill was here this morning. He said you were coming, but I never thought you would."

" Charlie ! When you were ill, did you think we could keep away ? "

"I don't know. You've kept away for half a year, isn't it? It seems like a hundred."

"That was my fault," said Sir Philip, in a deep voice unlike his own. "I thought you had disgraced us, and—now I find that it was for Flora's sake you suffered, and—— "

"Who told you?"—breathlessly, as a slight tinge of colour came into the wasted cheeks, and he shook with eagerness.

"The letters proved it. They were forgeries, every one of them."

"Forgeries!" With a gasp, he sank back on his pillow.

"Yes. You were Balfour's dupe; but now he shall pay for it, and you will be set free."

"Balfour! Free!" he murmured incoherently, the moisture gathering on his white face through excess of agitation.

One of the warders, who acted as nurse, stepped forward, and put a glass of something restorative to his parted lips.

"Yes, darling," said Flora, soothingly. "And as soon as the pardon comes, we will take you back with us to London, and nurse you so well that you will be strong as ever in a few weeks' time."

"It *would* be nice;" and he gave a little smile. It seemed as if his lips, so long attuned to sadness, had almost lost the power of framing a sign of joy. "But, don't be angry, I've prayed so hard to die—I think I shall."

"Oh no!" cried Flora, in a spasm of terror. "You *must* not, shall not, die! Oh, not till we have been happy together for a great many years; not till we have made up to you all the horrible pain of the last endless months! Think of Rose Dynevor, whose only hope in life is to see you free! Think of *me*!"

"Rose?" he repeated slowly, "was she sorry? Did she care?"

"Care! She nearly broke her heart; and she *will* break it, if you won't come back to her. Oh, Charlie, try to live, for her sake and mine!" She looked imploringly into his wasted face, and a tear trickled slowly down his cheek.

"I hope the pardon will be here by the end of the week," said Sir Philip, cheerfully. "Your friends have been working hard to clear you; and all the Foreign Office fellows will give you an ovation when you arrive in town. You must get up your strength, for I should not be surprised if you had to sign an affidavit before long."

"They are very kind. You must thank them."

"No; you shall thank them yourself. Come, Charlie, you must not disappoint us. Flora will have a capital time for nursing you before October, when we go to Paris. We have given

up Rome, so we shall always be at hand to look
after you, only just across the water."

A great longing came into the heavy eyes.
Life that had been so dismal, that the grave
looked bright in contrast, seemed fair enough
now to tempt him; but he could not in one
moment shake off the horror of months. The
shame and the bitterness had eaten into his
soul. Would Rose—would any one—speak to
him, with the felon's brand upon his skin?

"It was Rose who saw Captain Balfour
coming out of Philip's lodgings after you left,"
said Flora, trying to rouse him; "and it is her
great joy to think that her evidence will be of
use in clearing you."

"Would she care to notice me, after this?"
he said doubtfully.

"Of course she would! The story of your
noble self-sacrifice—oh, Charlie!"—and her lip
trembled—"it breaks my heart to think of it—
will make you a perfect hero in her eyes. She
has grown so quiet and sad, you would scarcely
know her; but your release will make her happier
than ever, and bring back the colour to her poor
white cheeks."

"But I have been a fool and a felon. Philip,
can they ever forget it?"

"No; but they will honour you for it, more
than any other man in England."

"And I could go back to my place at the office, without a stain ? "

"Without a stain; and G——, who knows the story, would be sure to promote you at once."

A great trembling came over him. Could he really take all this joy into his hands and grasp it ?

In his enfeebled condition any excitement was overpowering, and he lay back with closed eyes, utterly exhausted.

The doctor, who had entered unperceived, stepped forward and laid his finger on Charlie's pulse. "I think, in kindness to him, you had better retire," he said gravely. "After the enforced silence that is practised here, conversation of any kind is very trying."

Flora stooped to lay a kiss upon her brother's forehead.

"Good-bye," he murmured.

"Not good-bye, dear,"—with a sudden pang. "We are coming back to-morrow."

No answer; and so, with a long, loving look, she left the room, followed by her husband. A warder conducted them downstairs, as no visitors are allowed to wander about the place unaccompanied by some one belonging to the staff. The governor met them by the inner gate, and asked if they would care to walk round the

prison. Sir Philip accepted the offer readily;
so they were first taken to the chapel, where
service is held every week-day at half-past six,
and a second service on Sundays. It is a plain
building, but little ornamented, capable of holding a thousand people. The convicts sit on
benches on the ground floor, faced by a long row
of warders, and backed by a detachment of the
civil guard, with loaded rifles, ready for service
at a moment's notice. The two officers in
charge sit in square pews on either side, and
the rest of the officers in a gallery at the west
end.

"The harmonium is played by the school-
master, and the singing is unusually sonorous
from the number of male voices that join in it,"
said the major, leading the way across the wide
parade-ground to that part of the prison which
is called the dormitories.

Each of these dormitories contains sufficient
accommodation for two hundred convicts. The
cells run down the centre of an enormous room,
back to back. Every convict has a separate
cell; and Flora looked with tearful eyes at No.
382, and thought of the long hours of solitude,
silence, and despair that Charlie had passed
within its narrow compass. It was only seven
feet long—just one foot longer than his own
body—four feet wide, and seven feet high. A

hammock-bed, which when in use must have
nearly filled up the tiny room, was neatly rolled
up; two shelves, a board which might be
utilized as a desk, a hand-brush, and a basin,
composed the furniture; an aperture at the end,
and a space underneath the door, served as
ventilators; a single pane of semi-opaque glass
did duty for a window; and a hole in the door,
about the size of half a crown, was used as a
spy-hole by the warder in charge. The floor
was slate; the walls, or rather sides, of cor-
rugated iron; the door of wood.

It looked cheerless enough in summer; in
winter, the mere sight of it would chill you to
the bone.

The Trevellyans turned away in silence. No
wonder that Charlie had longed to die !

Major —— excused himself for not taking
them over the school, bake-houses, workshops,
etc., but he was obliged to leave them to see
after his duties. The convicts, in separate gangs,
were returning from their work, as, still under
the charge of a warder, they walked towards the
gateway. The privileged men wore breeches,
shirts, and waistcoats of blue serge, with red
arrows all over it, and small Scotch caps fitting
close to their heads; but the ordinary colour
worn by the larger number is dingy yellow,
striped with broad bands of grey. Flora shud-

dered as they passed, most of them with the
stoop of the hopeless in their bent backs, and
the sullen look of the despondent in their dim
eyes, as, staring straight before them, they went
by, without the energy or the interest to cast a
glance at the beautiful woman looking at them
so pitifully, as she pictured her brother in their
midst. Good God! to think of Charlie, with
close-cropped hair and that hideous garb, one
amongst that awful herd of human sheep!

"Let us go," she gasped. "This place gives
me the nightmare. I shall see it always in my
dreams."

CHAPTER XXII.

HOPE.

THE Trevellyans put up at the Bedford Arms, an imposing-looking hotel in the Elizabethan style, built on the foundations of the ruined abbey-house. The loquacious landlord entertained Sir Philip, when he strolled out into the garden to smoke his after-dinner cigar, with an account of the past glories of Tavistock Abbey, which was begun in obedience to a dream by Ordgar, Earl of Devon, in 961, and completed by his son, Ordulph the Giant, twenty years afterwards. But he scarcely cared to listen, as Mr. Smith pointed with pride to the old refectory, with its arched porch, just outside the garden walls, where, instead of tonsured monks gathering round a table with knives and forks, dissenters, whether bald or hairy, met together, Bible in hand, for a service of prayer.

Early the next morning they started for the prison, and through the kindness of the governor were allowed to proceed to the infirmary at once.

Charlie was asleep, and they stole softly to his bedside for fear of waking him. Perfectly motionless, except for the quick breathing, which raised his chest at irregular intervals, they were able to see more clearly than the day before how greatly he was altered. Of course there are few things more disfiguring than a moustache or beard cut roughly out of shape by a pair of scissors; but setting this aside, the face was scarcely recognizable. The consciousness of having done a noble deed had elevated his character, and his habitual expression of easy indifference had changed into one of endurance and resolution. The weakness had vanished, and so in a great measure had the beauty; but in its place there was something better, which showed to his loving sister, as she looked down on him with fondly admiring eyes, that, if he were only spared to her, she would no longer have to be the guide, the would-be Providence of her brother.

His eyes, opening slowly, looked straight into hers. "Then it wasn't a dream?"

"What, dear?"

"That you came yesterday; that—that—I am to be free?"

"No dream, but a blessed reality. Philip

and I will never rest till we can have you
with us."

" And the letters—you never wrote them ? "

" Balfour forged them," said Sir Philip, with
a frown.

" Ah ! "—with a deep breath of relief. " They
were the worst of all ! I got so dazed last
night, I could not tell if you had been here
really ; " and he held her hand in a tighter
grasp than the day before.

" I want you to tell me, in as few words as
possible, how it all happened. Tell me from the
beginning, when Balfour first gave you the
cheque."

Sir Philip sat down on the bed ; whilst Flora
knelt as before, with her head resting on the
pillow close beside her brother's.

With many halts between—for talking after
long months of silence is very tiring—Charlie
told his tale. Trevellyan hung on every word,
and took notes from time to time, afraid of
forgetting some detail of importance, the absence
of which might break the chain of evidence.

" I think we have enough, not only to clear
you, but to convict him," he said cheerily, as he
put his pencil and paper back into his pocket.
" It will be rather a joke, won't it, for you to
turn the tables upon him, and appear in the
witness-box against him ? "

A slight colour stole into Tremayne's cheeks.
"I could not do that," he said slowly.

A look of blank amazement came upon Sir
Philip's features. "In the name of Heaven,
why not?"

"Because he was once my friend. It may
be folly, but whatever he has done I can't
forget it."

"Folly! it's utter madness! The greater
your friendship, so much the greater his base-
ness. But we will let that be till you look a
little less washed out, and a little more fit to be
contradicted."

"Yes; we can afford to let Captain Balfour
wait," said Flora, gently. "Nothing will matter
when once you are free."

"Free!" he repeated, as if he loved the
word. "Free to come and go, to talk, to laugh,
as I used to do. Think, Flora; how many
months is it since I've heard the sound of a
laugh?"

She shivered. "Don't think of it. We shall
all be so happy in the future, that we shall
giggle from morning to night."

"Ravenhill is a good fellow," he said suddenly. "And I did him such injustice!"

"And me too," murmured Flora, as she hid
her blushing cheeks in the pillow.

"Yes; I know. It hurt me more than all

the rest. I think I should have gone mad "—
his lips trembled—" if it had not been for the
chaplain. You ought to shake him by the hand
before you go."

" We will be sure to look him up when we
come to fetch you," said Sir Philip ; " but we
cannot wait to-day. Come, Flora, the warder
says our time is up."

She raised her head, and threw her arms
round her brother's neck, looking long and
passionately into his face. " And when we
come, you will be strong and well, won't you ? "

" If I can ; " and he returned her look with a
smile, brighter than any which had lighted his
wasted face as yet, since prison walls had cast
their shadows over it.

" Good-bye for a few days," said Sir Philip,
grasping his hand. " Keep up your heart, and
soon we shall come back to carry you off."

" My love, my darling ! " murmured Flora.
" It's only for a short time—is it ? " With an
indescribable yearning in her heart, she tore
herself away and joined her husband. What if
the pardon should come too late—release to a
spirit that had flown !

They were just in time for the 12.29 train,
which steamed up to the platform as they drove
into the station yard. The journey home was
pleasanter than the journey down, when the

gloomiest forebodings had filled her mind; but
she could not help a lingering feeling of dread,
as she recalled her last look at Charlie's face as
he sank back, exhausted, after the agitating
interview.   His life seemed to hang on so frail a
thread that the slightest shock might break it.

It was not till they arrived at Yeoford
Junction that Sir Philip was able to procure
a paper, which gave but a very bald account of
the fête in the Botanical Gardens, and the
accident that had cast a shadow over its gaiety.
The first *Globe* that he captured, much nearer
to London, gave the right names, and he roused
Flora from her abstraction to listen to the
misadventures which had befallen her friends.

"Not a pleasant thing for Ravenhill to see
his wife's name coupled with Egerton's.   I
wonder if he is too absorbed to go after Charlie's
business?"

CHAPTER XXIII.

FORGIVEN.

BRENDA looked up eagerly into Lord Ravenhill's face, as he came into her boudoir, after passing the small portion of the night that was left after the accident, at Captain Egerton's lodgings. She had got up earlier than usual, in spite of her exhaustion, feeling that she could not rest in bed till she knew if Ronald were alive or dead. Now that her husband had come she did not dare to ask, and the question died on her lips.

"He is better; there is some chance of recovery, as the bullet has been extracted successfully, and the internal hæmorrhage has ceased;" and he threw himself down wearily in a chair.

Unable to control herself, Brenda burst into tears. He stretched his hand after the papers, which were lying on the table. Out of mere habit he took them up to read, though his

thoughts were busy with something else than
their print. He frowned as he heard his wife's
sobs, although his heart told him that they were
perfectly natural. If she had not shed a tear,
he would have accused her of want of feeling.

"Is he conscious? Does he know what has
happened? Is his brother with him?" she
asked between her sobs.

"He was conscious when I left, and Cuthbert was reading him to sleep. The love of
those two brothers for each other is something
wonderful; it goes to your heart." He stopped
abruptly.

"It shows that there is good in both of
them, doesn't it?"

"Yes; Cuthbert is as near perfection as a
man can be, and Ronald was a good fellow. He
had his faults, of course."

"Yes; but you were always fond of him,
weren't you?" she said earnestly. "He was
talking of you so kindly only last night."

"Last night under the willow?" and he
raised his eyes to hers searchingly, remembering
what he had seen, and wondering what he
might have heard if he had been nearer.

"Yes. But who is coming to nurse him?"
she asked, her thoughts reverting to his present
position.

"They have telegraphed for his mother;

and, meanwhile, Lady Grenville has installed herself as head nurse. I suspect Ronald would prefer not to change—between his mother and her two sons there is little sympathy."

"Poor fellow!" and her eyes filled with tears. It seemed so hard to sit there and do nothing for him, when instinct told her that the patient would have preferred her services to any other.

Lord Ravenhill knew what she must be thinking, and the thought angered him. He turned to his paper.

There was silence for some time. What had Captain Egerton meant by his hint of approaching departure? and what had made him so unlike himself for most of the preceding evening? Ruminating over these speculations, she lay quite still on the sofa, with her hands clasped, and her eyes shut. Presently she was startled by a loud exclamation from her husband, who crushed the newspaper in his hand and flung it on the carpet.

"Just as I expected—your name and his coupled together in every gossiping paper in the town!" He got up and planted himself on the hearthrug, his brows meeting over his flashing eyes. "By my soul! it is more than a man can stand!"

Brenda turned hot and cold in turn.

"To think that I cannot turn my back for a day and a half, without my wife compromising herself by her own extraordinary folly and disobedience!"

Deeply conscious of her fault, she hung her head in shame.

"If I had never warned you, it would have been different; but I had, and it was because I thought that I could trust you that I never spoke again." He went on with concentrated passion, "After that warning I should have no more thought of your going to a ball under his escort——"

"Edith was with me, and Bertie."

"Edith! a girl younger than yourself—about as capable of being a chaperone as a baby in arms; and Bertie, who is too giddy and light-headed even to take care of himself."

She did not attempt to defend herself. Slow tears trickled down her cheeks and into her lap, spoiling the ribbons which adorned the front of her *peignoir;* but she did not heed them. Her near approach to death had shaken her out of her morbid fancies; and she longed to be reconciled to her husband, longed to feel his sheltering arm cast round her, and to rest her weary head upon his heart, even whilst she told herself that she deserved his scorn.

Lord Ravenhill s position was to the last

extent exasperating. His indignation was just; and yet on either hand he was bound not to show it. The man who had injured him, as he thought, could scarcely be abused on his death-bed; and his wife, after her narrow escape from a horrible death, and plunged as she was into grief by Egerton's danger, seemed to have special claims upon his tenderness. He chewed the end of his moustaches in savage silence.

On reaching his home late the evening before, he had been enraged to hear that his wife had gone off to the Austrian fête without *him*, and with the man whose attentions she had promised to discourage. He followed as quickly as he could, hoping that his presence, however late, might stop the mouth of scandal. His ticket was on the mantelpiece in the library, so there was no difficulty about entrance, although the gatekeepers looked surprised at his plain evening suit, which he had been in no mood to give up for a fancy costume. Striding through the gardens with rapid steps, he soon reached the dancing tent, where he saw Edith Havergel waltzing with Godfrey Grenville. Brenda was nowhere to be seen. He turned away, determined to find her; but his search might have been long and tedious if Mrs. Muncaster, whose spirit of mischief never slept, had not spied him out,

and, creeping on tiptoe to his side, whispered
in his ear—

> "Love-birds seek a hidden nest—
> You will not find them with the rest;
> Beneath the willow's sheltering shade
> Love-vows are so quickly made."

She had gone before he could stop her; but
he recognized the voice, and hated it, even
whilst he acted on its suggestion. After wandering about in the semi-twilight of lamp-lit night,
he came upon the willow-tree, and saw Ronald
in the act of raising his wife's hand to his lips.
As he stepped forward in ungovernable fury, rage
was turned to horror, and horror to overmastering
grief; and he knew not whether to love or hate
the friend who was dying at his feet.

The same emotions were on him now—rage
fighting with sorrow, the friendship of boyhood
and manhood in one, protesting against the
fierce hatred of a recent hour. If Ronald
Egerton lived, he would know how to deal with
him; but if he died, he had no heart to desecrate
the peace of his grave.

His gloomy eyes rested doubtfully on his
wife. She looked so white and wan, with dark
circles under her eyes, no colour in her cheeks,
still wet with tears, and a pitiful expression of
woe in the drooping corners of her mouth. It
seemed the act of a savage to hurl reproaches

at a poor little head which bent so humbly to receive them; and yet how could he let such things pass by without a word, as if he were careless of his honour?

To Brenda, the silence became intolerable. All sorts of fancies came into her mind as to what her husband might be brooding over for her punishment, and her heart went down in closest proximity to her shoes. The most dreadful sentence might fall from his lips, if she could not soften his resentment before he spoke. In her desperation of extreme fear, she slipped from the sofa, and, creeping softly to his side, laid one imploring hand on his arm, and in a little feeble whisper said, "Forgive me."

Thrilled by the touch of her clinging fingers, and taken aback by her sudden humility, he hesitated. A great wave of tenderness poured over his generous heart at the first sign of repentance on her side; but was it not weak to yield? No matter; in moments such as these the heart must speak or burst.

He threw his arms round her—how she trembled, poor little thing!—and gathered her to his breast like a prodigal child. "I would have forgiven you long ago if you had only asked me," he said, with a catch in his breath, as he rested his cheek fondly on her soft brown curls. "Oh, child! why can't you love me as you did?" he

exclaimed impulsively, thinking of the worship
which she used to lavish on his unresponsive
self, before he knew where his own happiness
would eventually be centred.

"I did not think you cared," she murmured,
with her face buried in his coat.

"Not care! O God! what else is there to
care for on earth?" And he looked down at her
with eyes that spoke a whole volume of passion.
Basil did not love easily or often; but if he
loved at all, it was with the whole power of his
heart.

Shaking with a great bewildering happiness,
Brenda raised her head. There was no mistaking
the expression of her husband's eyes. With an
inarticulate cry, she threw her arms round his
neck. He loved her now, no matter what had
gone before, and her willing lips were raised to
his in a passionate ecstasy of satisfied doubt.
Heart to heart and lip to lip, there was no occasion for speech. More is said by action than
by word, when feeling stops the usually ready
tongue.

It was so easy to tell him everything now, as,
after an indefinite period of silence, they sat side
by side, and hand in hand, on the sofa. She
told him of her jealousy of Flora Trevellyan; of
her heart-breaking disappointment when Mrs.
Torrington hinted that she had been married

out of pity—here he frowned darkly as he pressed her hand, and murmured, " I loved you from the first ; " of her reckless resolution to amuse herself with other men, in order to wean her heart from him ; of her excessive anger when she thought that he was spending the time in the society of Flora that he could not spare to take her to the fête ; of her uncomfortable feelings, which had depressed her all the evening ; of Niederlohe's impertinence, at which Ravenhill scowled ; of Egerton's kindness and consideration—here his eyes fixed themselves on her with a glance of keen scrutiny ; of the warning uttered by the mask ; of her absurd burst of tears, and Ronald's eager defence of his friend.

" Why did you let him kiss your hand ? " he burst forth, unable to restrain himself as he recalled his indignation at the sight.

" How did you know ? " and the colour stole slowly into cheek and brow.

" I was there, and I saw it. I could have killed him at the moment."

" And yet you did your best to save him," she answered, with a smile. " He meant no harm by it. He was telling me that he was going away, and then he kissed it as a sort of farewell. It was the last time, he said "—her voice shook —" and so it may be."

" And so it will be, if he lives to a hundred.

Men shall learn to respect my wife behind my back, as well as before my face," he said resolutely. "And as for Niederlohe, he shall never put his foot inside my doors."

"I am sure I do not want him;" and she shivered.

"No; your promised cold shoulder did not have much effect. You must recollect, child"— he stroked her hair fondly to soften his words— "that men will measure their own conduct by yours. If you control them with too loose a rein, admiration may run away with discretion."

"I know; but I was so miserable. I didn't care." She hid her burning cheeks on his shoulder.

"As to this unfortunate business of last night, I scarcely know what is best. I was thinking over it, all the while I sat by Egerton's bedside. On the whole, I think it will be well for you to go quietly down to Beechwood. I had thought of Nice, but that is too far away. I should be in a fever if your letter missed a single post."

She raised her head in alarm. "But not alone? I couldn't go anywhere without you!"

Beechwood was the Ravenhill estate, a fine property in Sussex, to which Basil had taken his wife for the first time at Easter. The place had not been inhabited for some time, on account of the former Lady Ravenhill's weak health, which had forced her to live in a warmer climate than England, and Brenda had found it particularly depressing. She had a vivid remembrance of their first dinner-party—the stiff country people, who eyed her with curiosity, as if she had been a beast at a show, and had no conversation beyond their own narrow circle of interests; and a sprinkle of horsey young men, who could talk of nothing but past prowess with the hounds, or their prospective success in the steeplechases fixed for the following week.

"I should run down whenever I could," he said gently. "Even if you dislike it, I am afraid there is no help for it. After what happened last night, your name will be in every mouth, and much talk is fatal to a woman's reputation."

"But I can't go without you. Banishment is bad enough," and her eyes filled; "but solitude is unbearable."

"You shall have your sister for a companion. By-the-bye, where is she now?"

"I sent her down to the Haywards'. You know what Augusta is, and Edith thought it was better that she should hear the right version of last night, before she heard the wrong."

"She will be too late; it is in all the papers;" and his brows met.

"Not yet, surely?"

"Yes; you must be prepared for it. I daren't
show my face in the club, for I know they are
talking of nothing else down the whole length of
St. James's Street and Pall Mall. The next
thing will be that *Veracity* will get hold of it,
and make a capital story out of Beauty and the
Beast. It will fill a column and a half of the
Universe, make a fine cartoon in *Charivari*,
exhaust the unrivalled energies of the *Daily
Wire*——"

"Don't, Basil; I can't stand it."

"But you must," he answered sadly. "Those
who do wrong must pay for it; it is no use
grumbling over the coppers."

"But if you have forgiven it, what business
is it of theirs?"

"It is their province to provide an intellectual
feast for society; and they know that society
appreciates nothing so much as a dainty bit of
highly-flavoured gossip about the upper ten."

"But you won't let me go till he is better!"
Her eyes opened wide with eagerness, as she
thought what her feelings would be if she were
miles away, and did not know if Ronald were
alive or dead.

He hesitated. "I would let you know every
day."

"Oh, Basil, don't ask it;" and she clasped
her hands imploringly on his shoulder. "Think

how heartless and unfeeling it would seem to him, and he has been so good to me always. Don't send me yet."

"My darling"—the tender epithet was used to soften the bitter pill—"if it is for your good, it must be done."

And Brenda bowed her head, knowing that she of all people had no right to combat his will.

CHAPTER XXIV.

"I'M RIGHTLY SERVED."

"CUTHBERT, are you there?" said a voice, scarcely audible from excess of weakness, although the room was perfectly still.

Cuthbert Egerton bent over his brother with anxious eyes. "Are you better? Do you want anything?"

"Nothing; only to know about our friends."

"Lady Grenville is coming to see you to-morrow, and Sir Robert will probably look in to-night, whilst I am away."

"And Raven?"

"He was here this morning, only you were asleep." He could not withstand the question in those wistful eyes, so went on. "Lady Raven-hill has gone away"—the pale face grew paler still—"but she sent you those flowers, with her kind regards."

"Where?" and he tried to raise his head in eager search, but let it fall back on the pillow.

A bunch of white roses, fragile Souvenirs

d'Amitiés, was put into his hand. He looked at them fondly, then, when Cuthbert's back was turned, pulled them slowly and with difficulty up the counterpane, till he could touch them with his lips.

"How did they come?" He was hungry for every detail, and men were so sparing. If Lady Grenville had been there, she would have told him everything.

"Her husband brought them"—with a slight accent on the two first words, the nearest approach to anything like reproof that his brother could manage.

"Poor old Raven!"

For some time, Ronald lay perfectly still. The wind from the open window playing with his hair, and waving the ends of his moustaches —grown long through want of pruning. He was thinking, as his tired head had not been able to think for many days, and the result of his reflections seemed to be this—

"Look here, Cuthbert. I haven't injured him. I was wrong all through, I know, from the beginning."

A grave nod was the only answer.

"But I have done him no harm. She never cared for me, or it might have been different. Do you remember your sermon, and what I swore?"

"Yes; but why talk of it now?"

"The death of the unrighteous," he said musingly, with a far-off look in his eyes, as if he were gazing into a future, which slowly and sadly opened out before him. "It is rather like it, isn't it? Shot down like a dog."

"An accident like that may happen to any one. I dare say you might have escaped if you had been alone."

"I don't know if it would have occurred to me to run away. One's first idea in danger is to face it."

"If you have the pluck. No one will own to a deficiency in physical courage; but when it comes to a moral want, people are rather proud of it than not."

"Don't point your sarcasms at me," he said, with a faint smile, "but give me some liquor—look sharp."

Claret was the only wine that he was allowed to take; Cuthbert filled a tumbler with that and some iced water, and gave it to him, holding the glass as he drank it feverishly.

He gave a sigh of satisfaction, as he sank back on his pillows. "I can fancy the inhabitants of a desert picturing heaven simply as a land where they would have enough to drink. What can be more sublime than to drink when you are thirsty?"

"Go from the earthly to the heavenly, without a destruction of its spiritual meaning, and imagine the thirsty soul of men bathing in the waters of fruition. Think of it, Ronald," said Cuthbert, earnestly, as he refreshed his brother's burning forehead with eau-de-Cologne; "think of the craving 'for something afar,' which we all feel; think of desire dying in the light of perfect realization; think of hope folding her wings in the home which she has reached at last; think of heaven as the blessed place of rest, where all that is best in us will find its echo, where there will be no 'wishing and wanting,' with their wild unrest, no wearing, heart-breaking struggle after the unattainable, because the utmost limit of perfection will be reached."

The pale face glowed, the dark eyes shone, as if the young priest, already amidst the daily struggles of his self-denying life, were gladdened by a glimpse of the glory of a happier land beyond. But there was no response in the soldier's heart as yet; his mind, long occupied with the world and worldly things, could not jump at one bound from earth to heaven. An angel might beckon him, but nature still clave, with the tenacious hold of the drowning, to the fair things of earth, which were slipping from its grasp. They were present to him now, vividly present. He saw them directly he closed his heavy eyes, and nothing but the lethargic slumber of exhaustion could chase them from his mind.

He lay quite still, and Cuthbert thought he was asleep. Pulling out his watch, he found that he was due at his night school. If he could help it, he never liked to fail; but Sir Robert had not arrived, and he hesitated to leave Ronald alone.

"One question, old fellow, and then you can go," said Ronald, suddenly.

In a moment his brother was beside him. "I thought you were asleep."

"No. I've got a jolly lot of thinking to go through first;" and he smiled slightly. "But I can't get any peace till I am sure——" He stopped.

"Sure of what?"

"Sure that I haven't caused her a sorrow." The weak whisper was so low that it could scarcely be heard, but his eyes fixed themselves intently on Cuthbert's face, as if his very existence depended on his answer.

It was a cruel moment for Cuthbert. Absolutely truthful, deceit was impossible to him. He thought of Brenda's name hawked about in the gossip of the clubs; of the weekly papers, with their piquant travesty of the actual scene in the Botanical Gardens, which it was torture for the husband or wife to read; of Brenda's sudden banishment to a place she disliked—and hesitated.

Ronald turned his face to the pillow; the hesitation was answer sufficient. "I'm rightly served," he muttered, and closed his eyes.

* * * * *

His mother, Lady Campion, had come up in hot haste from Devonshire, only waiting to urge the Rev. Ebenezer Maguire to put up a special supplication at the next prayer-meeting, that "this dear but unholy brand might be plucked from the burning." On the way she caught a severe cold, which settled on her chest, and soon after her arrival, by the doctor's orders, was sent to bed, where she remained in the enjoyment of an attack of influenza; and where she was likely to stay, as Dr. Martin found that her fussy attentions and hypochondriac sighs were anything but beneficial to the patient. Cuthbert was the messenger between the two rooms, and she was continually lading him with a heap of tracts, which he looked at from down his nose, and scarcely liked to touch with the tips of his fingers. He was too conscientious not to deliver them; but Ronald generally told his man to remove them at once, and sent a message to his mother that they were very useful—and forgot to add, in lighting the kitchen fire. His father was engaged in some scientific explorations amongst the Rocky Mountains, and, if he did not tumble down a precipice beforehand, would probably return when he heard of his son's illness.

Cuthbert was glad that there was no one, not even a father or mother, to stand between him and his brother. His love for him was so great and so *exigeant*, that he wished to do everything for him, and grudged—as far as it was in his kindly heart to grudge—the smallest service performed by another. In all his life he had never had so hard a struggle with his conscience as now. When he gave up the privileges of his position in the world, all the pleasure and the pride, which have such alluring charms for budding manhood, and brought down on his back the bitter reproaches of an angry mother, the contempt of a worldly-minded father—when he was made an unwelcome intruder in his own home, and had the cold shoulder turned on him by most of his family, simply because he knew his duty, and accepted it—then the struggle had been bitter, God only knew how hard! but the reward had been so sure in the bit of good, however small, that it would be his blessed office to do to his fellow-creatures. Then resignation was easy, and every day of patient progress against evil brought a ray of comfort to his heart. Now, face to face with the sorrow that was to rob him of his only bit of sunshine, it was impossible. Sinners are apt to think that goodness is easy, and comes with as little pain as second teeth to those who lead a holier life than theirs. They know nothing of the hard struggles and the many tears that it costs, even to the best of mortals. They judge by the effect, and ignore the means.

Like a rose to the summer, sunshine to the day, Ronald, the bright, daring soldier, was to his graver brother his crown of joy. The love of woman had never made Cuthbert's pulses beat with a warmer glow; all the best affections of his heart were twined round his brother, all his earthly hopes fixed on the success of his career. In an imperious but most loving fashion of his own, Ronald had ruled him, looking after his health and worldly welfare with a tenderness that was surprising in a butterfly of fashion, and savoured more of a woman than a man. Even in the matter of going to the south of France, he knew that, if all had gone well, Ronald would probably have carried him off; for he was weak to resist when his brother insisted, and a refusal might bring a cloud to the fair, frank face where smiles were more frequent than frowns.

O God! was it possible that, when August came, the one so full of life, and hope, and happiness would be cut off in the flower of his

strength; and the other, frail and delicate, left
to toil alone in fevered alleys and poverty-
stricken homes, with no smile to brighten his
dull lodging, no kindly voice to bid him good
cheer after a day of care?

It *could* not be true! With untiring patience,
he set sums, wrote copies, corrected spelling;
and then, when the night-school was over, he
went back to his own rooms in solitude and
prayer to fight out the battle with his rebellious
heart. The flesh was terribly weak, and the
spirit unwilling, but he *knew* that God's way
must be best, be the sacrifice what it might
to us who suffer. And when, one hour later, he
stepped into the street, those who looked into
his steadfast face might have known that he had
conquered.

Every earthly tie in severance weans us more
from earth to heaven; and, hugging this truth
to his desolate heart, he had got beyond the
fret and fume of grief to the infinite peace of
resignation.

CHAPTER XXV.

" SI TU SAVAIS ! "

" AND he is better—really better ? " said Brenda, anxiously, as she paced up and down the terrace at Beechwood, with both hands clasped on her husband's arm.

Mrs. Havergel and Mary were seated under the cedar-tree on the lawn; Edith was playing lawn-tennis with Bertie Fitz-herbert at a little distance, and the excited manner in which they kept calling out the score, as if they wished all things animate and inanimate to be cognizant of the wavering chances, showed that they were absorbed in the game.

" Better ? Of course he is," said Lord Ravenhill, cheerfully. " I actually made him laugh when I told him of De Zinsky's pathetic lament over the dead lion—' slaughtered to save the life of an aristocrat.' If it had been *vice versâ*, I don't think he would have objected."

" Much obliged to him. Did he forget that I was there as well ? "

"Not quite, because he was polite enough to come and inquire, like the rest of the world, after your health."

They stood still to admire the prospect, which was certainly fine, in spite of Brenda's prejudice. Several stately cedars on the wide-spreading lawn at their feet lent an air of sombre grandeur to the gardens, which were flanked on either side by long shrubberies, which developed into woods, and shielded the intervening space from every breath of the east or west winds. The house was square, with turreted windows, but not a single creeper adorned its nakedness, not an ivy leaf lent grace to its solidity. The beds on the lawn were bright with geraniums, calceolarias, foliage plants, etc.; but the lawn lay so much lower than the terrace, with which it communicated by flights of steps at either end, that when Brenda arrived the week before, not a flower was to be seen from the drawing-room windows. The gardeners received immediate orders to remedy the want. The rooms were filled with bloom, and bouquets of bright blossoms were placed in the stone vases along the parapet. Creepers were to be planted as soon as possible, and next year the place might look almost cheerful; but at present it seemed to Brenda, fresh from the gaieties of the London season, a dreary hole, whose only recommendation was its size.

Beyond a pleasant range of green pastures, there was a slow, steady-going river, bordered with a tufted fringe of alder and willow; beyond the river, rose the softly rounded hills, looking blue in the shadows; behind the hills was the setting sun, tingeing their summits with its dying glories. A sheep-bell tinkled in the fields; a girl's voice, mellowed by the distance, called the dun-coloured Alderneys to be milked; a bird twittered to its mate, and Brenda sighed.

"What is the matter, child?" and her husband laid his hand fondly upon hers.

"Nothing. Only whenever I look at a sunset, I think of death; and so often lately I have been afraid for Captain Egerton."

"But you needn't be any longer. Dr. Martin was quite cheery this morning, when I called round on my way to the station. To-morrow I intend to take him up a basket of fruit, and you may send him some more flowers."

"I will," she said softly.

Basil was silent for some time, thinking of his last interview with Ronald, when the poor fellow had begged his forgiveness for all the trouble and annoyance he had cost him. He knew of his intention of throwing up his appointment at the Horse Guards, and joining his old battalion at Marseilles, on the way to India; and, fully appreciating his motive, he had re-

turned his grasp with a silent pressure that tried
the weak man's strength, but soothed his mind.
If it had not been for certain reasons, he would
have told him, when a little stronger, to come
down to Beechwood and be nursed back into
health; but, for Ronald's own sake, it was better
that he should go away. After a year or two of
absence, he would come back cured of his foolish
fancy, and settle down into the quiet, steady
friendship which lent a sweetness without a
sting to life.

Brenda's voice roused him from his reverie.
" When you see him to-morrow, will you tell
him how much we all think of him? It seems
so dreadful for him to be prisoned in a sick-room
in all this glorious weather."

He looked down at her doubtfully. There
was sorrow in her face, but sorrow lying at the
top of joy, as if even sympathy with a friend in
distress could not spoil her new-found bliss.
Yes, it was safe to tell her.

" He sent you a message, Brenda."

" Did he? What is it?" The blood rushed
into her cheeks like a sudden reflection of the
sunset.

" ' Ask her to forgive me.' What for, I did
not ask."

" There is nothing—no reason at all," she
said hurriedly. " I suppose he means all this

tiresome fuss in the papers, and that kind of thing; but it was my fault, not his. And he behaved like an angel. Basil, you will tell him so, *won't* you? When you are ill, things weigh on your mind; and I shouldn't like any uncomfortable thought about me to trouble him."

"I will tell him that you have nothing to forgive, as a message from you;" and his tone was grave.

"Yes; and tell him that I sent him those Souvenirs d'Amitié, to show that there was to be no difference in our friendship. I may say that, mayn't I?"

"Through me, perhaps; not otherwise."

The dressing-bell rang. Mrs. Havergel shut up her book, and came slowly across the lawn, followed by Mary.

"A lovely evening," she said, with a smile, as she met the husband and wife, "but so oppressive; it must be especially trying for the sick."

"Yes; especially the sick in a district like Cuthbert Egerton's. Fancy a day like this spent in the bosom of your family, and in a room eight feet square, reeking of smoke, and filth, and red herrings!"

"But every one doesn't eat herrings," said Brenda.

" Half the poor of London feed upon bloaters;
but you can diversify them if you like by a dish
of savoury tripe and onions, or anything equally
gratifying to the patient's nose. Bertie," he
shouted, " time for dinner! We won't wait for
them," he said, with a smile, as he pushed
open the French doors into the drawing-room.
" Punctuality is the virtue of middle age, and
youth knows nothing about it."

The rector came in to dinner, and the
evening passed pleasantly with conversation and
music. Bertie told some amusing stories of his
Addiscombe days, at which Edith laughed
merrily; whilst the Rev. Arthur Agnew gave
some witty sketches of his more eccentric
parishioners, which delighted his host. Mrs.
Havergel listened with a placid smile. Relieved
of her anxiety about her daughter, her heart
was lighter than it had been for years; and
released from all home worries and domestic
cares, she was determined to enjoy her brief
holiday whilst she could. Mary was diverted by
Bertie's fun, and joined in it every now and
then, not seeing why she should leave it all to
her younger sister, who seemed to be losing her
heart at the same time as her gravity. Brenda
alone was sad. An unconquerable depression
was upon her. It reminded her of her feelings
at the Austrian fête, and she could not free

herself from the idea that some misfortune was impending.

She played; but her music was all of the plaintive sort, and most of the melodies were in a minor key. Anything lively seemed to jar, in the present subdued tone of her spirits.

"Sing us that old song with which you enchanted Duplessis," said Lord Ravenhill, throwing down his evening paper, and coming to turn over her music.

Rather unwillingly she began. Her sweet voice rang through the room, quivered, and broke.

"I am hoarse to-night," she said hastily, as a big lump rose in her throat, and, getting up from the stool, she crossed the room quickly, and went out on the terrace.

"*Si tu Savais!*" How clearly she had read those words in Ronald's eyes before he bent down to kiss her hand! She leant her elbows on the parapet, and looked wistfully at the impassive moon, shining in such peaceful majesty across the silent sky. Could there be no happiness without its counterside of pain? Must the joy of one be the grief of the other? The truth came to her as she stood there in the silent night; and with sorrow and humility she saw into the honest heart, which she had played with so recklessly. Her own was full of happiness in its restored confidence in her husband's love; but a shadow was cast over its joy through sympathy with her friend.

* * * * *

"If you only knew how sorry I am!" she sighed to the one whose ears were longing for the sound of her voice; and the moon answered back with a cold sad smile, as if it knew how futile woman's sorrow was—when too late.

CHAPTER XXVI.

ALAS! FOR RONALD EGERTON.

"You will go to France, old fellow; promise me that," said Ronald, waking up from a long stupor.

"We will go together, or not at all;" and Cuthbert's brow contracted, as his eyes rested with yearning affection on his brother's face.

Was ever countenance so fitted to win the love of woman, or the friendship of man? The broad honest brow; the fearless eyes, which could flash fire in a moment of anger, and soften so winningly when his brief wrath had passed; the sweet-tempered mouth, shaded by a fair moustache, once curled with the care of a dandy, now long and drooping, like its owner's strength; the ready smile, which even in illness was so prompt to return when pain had lessened —would there ever come a time when he would see them only in his dreams? Could he live to face it, if it came?

"You must go. London's like an oven, and you are wasting to skin and bone."

"If I am, so much the better." The unwonted bitterness was the outcome of his pain.

"Look here, Cuthbert, I'm serious for once in my life;" and he tried in vain to raise himself on his elbow, to lend force to his words. "Wherever I go, I couldn't rest, if I knew that you were coughing your heart out with no one to look after you."

"And do you think I should care? Do you think I shall want to last for ever, when—when—— O God! my brother, it seems more than I can bear!" and utterly carried beyond his usual self-control, Cuthbert buried his face in the counterpane.

For a long, long time there was silence in presence of a sorrow too deep for words.

All through the long oppressive day, Ronald's strength was waning. The doctors came, shook their heads, and went softly out of the room, wondering at the sudden relapse after the improvement of the day before. Champagne was substituted for claret, and the patient was to have anything in the way of nourishment that he fancied. Unfortunately, he fancied nothing except a little fruit to soften his fevered mouth. Straw was laid down all the length of Albemarle Street, and the knocker was muffled, so there

were no outside noises to disturb his fitful sleep,
although brother-officers and friends of every
description besieged the door. Daintily dressed
women stepped out of their carriages at the
corner, fearful even of the very slight sound
that wheels can make on straw, and, with tears
in their eyes, made their inquiries and left their
offerings of fruit or flowers from their own hot-
houses and conservatories.

Regretted by all, he was forgotten by none.
Even Niederlohe, who liked him but little as the
more favoured friend of Lady Ravenhill, came
to ask after him, and left a card, which card, on
being presented to Ronald, he quietly tore to
pieces with his teeth, as a token of what his
crippled right arm would like to do to its owner.
Ah me! some one else would have to chastise
the Austrian, if he ever offended again!

Lady Grenville came late in the day, and
took up her position by the bedside. She had
known Egerton ever since he first joined his
regiment, and, in spite of the anxiety he had
caused her on Brenda's account, she had grown
to care for him as if she had been his elder
sister. She knew that no one but a woman
could nurse a patient properly, or else, in spite
of her affection, she might have left him to
Cuthbert's care with perfect confidence, if only
his strength had been equal to his love.

Ronald's mind wandered continually. He was a boy at Eton, hitting to right and left in a cricket match whenever he got a chance of a ball, which the bowler seemed slow to send; or else he was shooting partridges in Devonshire, or trying to hit them, for he generally failed, and his gun was loaded with the wrong shot. And sometimes he would call "Brenda! Brenda!" in a voice of entreaty which went to his listeners' hearts, and listen and yearn for an answer which never came. Then he would turn to his pillow, and hide his face with an endless sigh; and the tears rolled down Beatrice Grenville's face for very sympathy.

The rays of the setting sun, which Brenda was watching with her husband at Beechwood, poured in through the open window and lighted up the patient's face with sudden radiance. "I think she hears," he whispered to himself, and softly fell asleep.

Lady Campion was called in haste. Wrapped in a dressing-gown, she came in with her handkerchief to her eyes.

"You frightened me so," she said querulously, after one glance at the sleeper. "I thought he was worse."

She was a tall, delicate-looking woman, with sickly complexion, regular features, and dark hair, more like Cuthbert than Ronald, but with such a widely different expression that the likeness was scarcely noticeable.

"Who was he calling out to just now? It sounded like a woman's name," she asked in a whisper, as she sat down in the chair which Lady Grenville resigned to her.

"It was a lady whom he was very fond of?"

"You think he is really bad, do you?"

"As bad as bad can be," said Lady Grenville, sadly.

"Then let her be sent for, if she is within reach. Quick, Cuthbert, if you know her address. Poor boy! let him have his last wish;" and she began to cry hysterically.

The two others exchanged glances. Cuthbert shook his head, but Lady Grenville nodded resolutely.

"A good-bye," she said in a trembling voice, "ought never to be refused to the dying."

And he yielded.

A telegram was despatched at once. On consulting a time-table, they found that there was a train from Beechhill, the nearest station to Beechwood, at ten o'clock, which reached Charing Cross soon after eleven. If Lord Ravenhill consented to bring her, Brenda might reach Albemarle Street before the half-hour, and those who knew his generous heart felt sure he would not refuse.

The minutes passed slowly. The dinner
hour was passed without notice, nine sounded
from a distant clock, and the sleeper stirred
uneasily.

Cuthbert knelt down and read the prayers
for the sick. His voice, usually clear as a bell,
was hoarse with suppressed feeling; but with a
manful effort he constrained his bursting heart
to calmness, whilst he prayed for his brother's
soul. Solemnly the holy words sounded through
the hushed room. They seemed like the cooling
touch of chilly fingers on a burning head, and
brought a restful peace to troubled breasts.

At half-past nine, when Brenda was standing
on the terrace and thinking of him with sad
regret, Ronald opened his eyes. He looked at
them all in turn, and smiled.

Lady Campion, sobbing wildly, buried her
face in his pillow. She had not recognized his
danger until this evening, and the blow was
overpowering. She might have been so much
to him, her bright, beautiful boy, and she had
been so little, thinking more of her narrow
creeds and prejudices than of all the wide range
of her maternal duties. Death seemed impossible for Ronald, the strong, healthy fellow,
who had never known a day's illness in his life.
Cuthbert was different, he had been ailing from
his youth; and yet Death chose the strong, and

left the weak. Where was consolation to be found? And who could fill the gap when he had gone?

Mother, brother, and friend—he parted from them all with loving words; but still the wistful eyes roved round the room, as if seeking for some one who was not there.

Lady Grenville bent down to hear the whisper.

"Is she coming?"

"Yes."

"Tell her"—the feeble breath was failing fast—"that I'm glad to die;" and then the tired head fell back, the blue eyes closed, and, with a slight smile on his lips, he slept like a weary child, with his hand fast clasped in his brother's.

A carriage drove up to the door; quick steps came up the stairs, and, with her husband by her side, Brenda stood with awestruck hesitation on the threshold of the darkened room.

Too late! The eyes that had sought for her were closed; the ears that had listened for her would hear no more; the voice that had called for her was silent; and the good-bye was hushed on lips that would never speak for weal or woe again.

Ronald was dead!

CHAPTER XXVII.

SUSPENSE.

ON their arrival in London, the Trevellyans found a note in Lord Ravenhill's handwriting, which proved that he had not forgotten his promise to look after Charlie's affairs, in spite of the tragic incident which had happened in the evening. Mrs. Lloyd had been interrogated on the subject of her visitor on the night of Tremayne's arrest; and finding that it was for the dear young gentleman's interest that the fact should be known, she had openly avowed that Balfour had been to his room, and that, peeping in at the door to see what he was about, she saw him draw some papers out of his pocket, and place them in the desk. With many tears, she confessed that she had only sworn to the contrary because the Captain had told her that it would be for Mr. Tremayne's good that nothing should be known of his visit.

After this, there were many consultations

with Mr. Goodeve, who prepared the evidence
for the Home Secretary. Alphonse Dupont,.
former valet to Sir Philip, and only temporarily
discharged on account of ill health, proved that
Captain Balfour had been in Sir Philip's room
on the 18th of December, after Mr. Tremayne
had left it, or certainly at the same time, as he
heard their voices, whilst he was packing up his.
master's things in the adjoining bedroom. The
counsel for the prosecution had not been in-
structed to examine him on this point, so he had
not mentioned it at the trial. The gatekeeper
at the Foreign Office proved that the cheque for
two thousand pounds had been given by Balfour
to Tremayne. Lionel Westmacott proved that
the two five-pound notes had been borrowed
from some one at Victoria, and he saw Captain
Balfour leave the station soon afterwards. Abel
Macniece, keeper of the Rose and Crown, Wych
Street, Covent Garden, affirmed that a man
resembling Captain Balfour, but with red hair,
changed one of the notes, which were subsequently
stopped on the evening of the 2nd of January.
James Bryant deposed that a man, whom he
afterwards identified as Captain Balfour in St.
Pancras's Church, bought a red wig, and whiskers
and beard to match, at his shop on the 2nd of
January. Captain Whittaker deposed that
Captain Balfour, when travelling down to Bed-

ford with him on the 4th of January, declared
that he was soon going to claim his bride, as he
had got sufficient money for the settlements.
He thought at the time that his brother officer
was the worse for drink.   The tailor's bill, afterwards found in Charlie Tremayne's desk, belonged
to him, and had been missed by him shortly
after a visit from Captain Balfour. He could
not have given it to Tremayne himself, as he
had never spoken to him in his life.   Mrs.
Lloyd's deposition followed. Miss Rose Dynevor
stated that she had seen Captain Balfour
come out of Sir Philip Trevellyan's lodgings
after Charlie Tremayne had left. Messrs.
Hardcastle and Flint, bankers, King William
Street, affirmed that the sum of four thousand
pounds had been placed to Captain Balfour's
account towards the middle of the month of
January. The criminating papers were proved
to be written on the same notepaper as that
which Captain Balfour was in the habit of pur-
chasing at F. Robinson's, stationer, High Street,
Bedford. Mrs. Smithson, landlady of 28, Tavistock Street, where Captain Balfour often took a
lodging, stated that several nights in the beginning of the new year, when, being restless with
the toothache, she could not stay in bed, she had
seen a light under the captain's door so late as
five in the morning, and on peeping through the

keyhole, had found that he was busy writing. She had never known him write so late before. Her servant found a piece of yellowish paper with the name of Trevellyan written repeatedly upon it, pushed under the fender, and brought it to her to see if it were of any importance. The forged letters were brought forward as sufficient reason for Tremayne's silence, and also as proof that Captain Balfour had a strange facility in copying other people's handwriting.

The evidence of Miss Dynevor and Alphonse Dupont proved that Captain Balfour had perjured himself at the trial; the alleged letters of Lady Trevellyan made it equally evident that he would not hesitate to commit the crime of forgery if he had an adequate object in view.

All this mass of evidence, well sifted, tested, and prepared by Mr. Goodeve, was laid as soon as possible before the Home Secretary; who applied to Baron Brown, for his advice. The Baron, on referring to his note, found that he had alluded, in the course of his summing up, to the discrepancy between the witness of Mrs. Lloyd, the landlady of 200, Jermyn Street, and Mary Ann Leeson, the maidservant. That point was now cleared up by the subsequent admission of Mrs. Lloyd. The chief difficulty that the defence had to meet, was the silence of the prisoner as to the source from which he obtained

the cheque. That silence was now broken, and
the forged letters fully explained its motive.
The presence of Captain Balfour during, and
after, the visit of Tremayne to Trevellyan's
lodging, was a decided point in the prisoner's
favour, and against Balfour. On the whole, the
Baron inclined to a belief in Tremayne's innocence.

Whilst the Home Secretary was consulting,
analyzing, and picking to pieces all the evidence
before him, a detective was sent down to Bedford
to watch the movements of Captain Balfour, in
case he might take it into his head to leave the
country.

Flora Trevellyan was nearly wild with suspense. A few days lost in deliberation might
cost her brother's life. The doctor had told her
plainly that if it had not been for the sudden
hope of release, which had given the required
stimulus to his vital powers, he must have sunk
through weakness, increased as it was by dejec-
tion. If the wretched lawyers were too long in
making up their minds, Charlie might actually
die before the pardon was sent.

Lady Jemima Broadbent, roused into activity
by her nephew's misfortune, gave Sir Philip and
Lord Ravenhill no peace. She threatened to go
to Whitehall and bully the Home Secretary into
an immediate answer. She scolded them all

round for their dilatoriness, and vowed that if the matter had been placed in her hands, Charlie would no sooner have been shut up, than shut *out.* Sir Philip, impatient to the last degree himself, was nearly goaded into frenzy by her aggravating reproaches, and told her at last to go to Windsor, or to Hades if she liked; but to let the Home Secretary alone, or she might ruin everything.

There was some one else who must not be forgotten, whose every wish and hope in life seemed to hang on the issue of the next few days; one whose young heart was very weary of waiting, and sick with the longing of hope deferred—Rose Dynevor. Surely the day of sorrow had lasted long enough, and in God's own Word came the promise, "In the evening time there shall be light."

CHAPTER XXVIII.

AT LONG LAST.

HER Majesty graciously condescended to pardon
Charles Tremayne for being imprisoned on a
false charge in the convict establishment of
Princetown, Dartmoor, in the county of Devon.
The pardon, duly signed and sealed, was already
on its way, when a notification of the fact from
the Home Secretary was handed to Sir Philip
Trevellyan, as he sat at breakfast, with his wife
in Queen Anne's Gate.

He looked up with sparkling eyes. Come
at last!" he said simply, as he threw it across
the table; but none the less his heart gave a
great bound of joy, and on pretence of fetching
himself a cup of tea, he got up.

"Oh, Philip!" was all she said, but tears of
thankfulness were raining down her cheeks, as
she leant her head against his coat. Excessive
joy is rarely boisterous; but that one quiet
minute of unbounded, overflowing happiness obli-

terated half a year of sorrow. Her heart rose in gratitude to God. How could she ever pay Him back by a whole life of devotion for such goodness as this!

Sir Philip cleared his throat. "We must start at once to fetch him." She raised her head eagerly. "It is just upon eleven now; but the 11.45 only gets there at the same time as the 2.15 express, so we may as well go by that."

"Oh, what a time to wait!" Nevertheless she pushed away her chair, as if they were to start directly.

"Mayn't I have some more tea?" he asked with a smile. "I don't see why you should starve either me or yourself, because we are going on a long journey."

She filled his cup, and rose from her seat.

"You have eaten nothing," he remonstrated.

"This is meat and drink to me," she replied with shining eyes, pressing the Home Secretary's precious effusion to her heart.

"You will faint, and I shall leave you behind," he observed, as he resumed his seat as if nothing had happened. "But, seriously, Flora, there are a good many things to be thought of. He must have a decent suit of clothes to put on before he leaves the prison.

"I know that; they are ready."

"Bravo! Nothing like a woman for thinking

of details. We shan't get down till 8.19, and in his weak state he can't possibly travel all night."

"Of course not;" and she leant against the back of a chair with a happy smile. "I have arranged everything in my own mind, so nicely. He will sleep at the Bedford Arms, Tavistock, to-night, to-morrow at Exeter, and the next day, or the day after, we bring him up to town."

"So that is the programme; I hope we shall carry it out," said Sir Philip, quietly cracking the shell of another egg.

"I think Etienne had better go with us."

"I don't think I shall want him."

"Perhaps not; but Charlie will. He must be properly shaved before he shows his face."

"To Miss Dynevor?"—slily.

"To any of his friends"—with a glance of reproof. "His moustaches were like a tooth-brush."

"And Rose might object to be scrubbed."

"He used to be good-looking," she answered gravely, "and I don't want any one to see him so spoilt."

"Fortunately, cropped hair is the fashion. I think I owe it to Ravenhill to tell him of this, at once," he added more seriously.

And Flora nodded her warm approval before

she left the room to make the necessary arrangements for the journey.

* * * * *

Five days later, a knot of friends gathered on the platform at Waterloo Station. There was Lord Ravenhill, with some of the sadness caused by the death of Ronald Egerton banished for the present from his handsome face, in natural satisfaction at the complete success of his efforts on behalf of Charlie Tremayne; the Master of Strathrowan, tranquil as usual, carrying out his *rôle* of universal benefactor by hanging on his own arm the basket of oranges which belonged to a pretty girl in a shabby ulster, who eyed him suspiciously, having an idea that he meant to walk off with her property; Godfrey Vivian, who had taken to wear his hat with the peculiarly knowing swagger of an actor, because his divinity had gone on the stage; Lionel Westmacott, whose labours at Washington were always about to begin in the course of the next fortnight; and little Peere Sylvester, looking pathetically patient, as Westmacott placed himself in front of him and poured out an anecdote, which he did not want to hear, about the Khedive's slippers.

"Rather late," said Basil, after consulting his watch.

"Yes, rather," was the Master's laconic answer.

"Not rather," objected Vivian, "but very late indeed—ten minutes behind time; it is nearly half-past five. We'll bring an action against the directors for the loss of our precious time, due, I can swear, to the Government."

"Who asked you to lose it?" inquired Strathrowan.

"Lady Trevellyan." Basil turned round quickly. "That is to say," he added lamely, "I know she would be terribly disappointed if she did not see me here."

"Perhaps she won't see you——"

"By Jove! here they are!" cried Sylvester, craning his neck round his tormentor's tall form.

With a scream and a puff, the engine slipped past them. Sir Philip's fair head protruded from the window of a first-class carriage. There was a general rush to the door, which was thrown open by eager hands, before the train had come to a standstill. Trevellyan stepped out, followed by Flora, who, without noticing any of her friends, turned at once, with outstretched arms, to assist her brother. Slowly, and with difficulty, one weak leg came after the other till their owner stood upon the platform, with a look of bewilderment in his blue eyes. They crowded round him, grasping his hand with hearty congratulations, and almost pulling him to pieces in their eagerness.

Nearly overpowered, he leant upon Sir Philip's arm, the tears in his eyes and his lips quivering.

"Glad to see you back, old fellow!"

"Wish you joy, 'pon my word!"

"We've missed you horribly at the F.O.!"

"I swore the States shouldn't see me till you were free!" cried Westmacott.

"Dear friends, you are all so kind," said Flora, between laughing and crying; "but you must let him go now. He has been ill, and can't stand much."

"The carriage is here. I suppose your people are looking after your luggage?" said Ravenhill. "Let us lead the way." And they went forward.

"I say, Tremayne," cried Vivian, "all London is mad about the Modern Martyr. There's an awful crowd outside."

Charlie looked up in alarm. "Not really?"

"Never mind; we will be your bodyguard," said Sylvester, with the usual courage of the tiny.

Vivian spoke the truth. As soon as Tremayne appeared, frantic cheers rose from the throng outside. The news of his arrival spread from street to street, and every minute served to augment the crowd, as new-comers rushed up in breathless haste.

Nervous and bewildered at finding himself such an object of interest, Tremayne hurriedly stepped into the carriage with bent head, and hid himself in the corner. Hats, hands, and handkerchiefs waved on every side, deafening shouts rent the air, and, amidst a tumult of welcome, the landau drove off; the horses, startled by the noise, kicking and rearing, added to the excitement.

Some of the crowd lingered to read with renewed interest the staring placards stuck up outside the station—"Great Miscarriage of Justice;" "Release of Charles Tremayne;" "Journey from Dartmoor," etc., etc.,—and the four friends walked back, arm in arm, to Downing Street.

Lord Ravenhill, having received the only reward he craved, which was to see Flora Trevellyan's lovely face radiant with smiles instead of blanched with tears, walked homewards to Grosvenor Place, knowing that Brenda would be looking out for him and anxious to hear the news.

Arrived at Queen Anne's Gate, Charlie Tremayne was placed upon the sofa in Flora's private sitting-room, and after having had a suitable stimulant administered to him by his sister's hands, and prepared by his brother-in-law, he was told to keep quiet.

"Don't go," he remonstrated, solitude being the last boon he wished for, as they both walked towards the door.

"We are coming back presently," said Sir Philip, with a nod, as he went out, followed by his wife.

Left to himself, Charlie looked round the pretty room with appreciative eyes. No one could tell the really æsthetic refreshment of seeing all the pretty knickknacks of statuettes, pictures, china, and all sorts of graceful *bric-à-brac*, after the utter bareness of his cell. He was feasting on them placidly, when the door opened, the curtain was pulled aside, and a small figure, clothed in soft grey cashmere, stood on the threshold.

"Rose!" he said wonderingly, and tried to raise himself on his elbow. She seemed to hesitate, as if too frightened to enter. "Oh, *do* come in and speak to me."

Slowly, as if with half a mind to fly, she came forward.

"I can't get up, so in charity come close!" he entreated.

And, in pity to his weakness, she came so very near that, with a sudden accession of strength, he was able to draw her gently towards him.

"They say you haven t forgotten me?" and

he looked straight into her blushing face, his heart beating like twenty.

"Never!" she whispered, with a shy smile; and then lips and hearts seemed to meet at the same moment, with all the passion of a love that had waited, and pined, and despaired, gathering strength with every obstacle that tried to crush it out.

To Charlie Tremayne, ex-convict and pardoned felon, it was as if all the suffering and the sorrow of the past were condoned by the rapture of a kiss. Surely in this world of woe, one moment of perfect joy, even when bought by six months of despair, is wondrously cheap at the price.

CHAPTER XXIX.

"DESPAIR."

THE funeral was over. Mr. Ward, utterly broken-hearted, had stood beside his son-in-law at his daughter's grave, sobbing like a child, every sod of earth that fell seeming to make the separation more complete between him and his Kate. There were several of his daughters with him; but their grief was not like his. *They* might marry and have children of their own, with ever-widening circles of interest; but for him there was no future, except in theirs, and the best, and the fairest, and the better loved than all, had been taken from him, and the gap that she left, nothing and no one could ever fill. There would always be something wanting, something missing, till he was able to join her in a better world than this.

"Balfour has no more heart than a stone," he said to himself, with a frown, as they returned together in the melancholy vehicle which is supposed to add solemnity to a funeral procession.

And Balfour felt as if his heart were really a stone ; but not, as his father-in-law imagined, through want of feeling, but rather through its excess. The blow had literally stunned him, and every sentiment, whether of sorrow, or remorse, or fear, was in abeyance. To-morrow or the day after he might come to life, as it were, and feel the pain that the miserable father felt, only redoubled in its intensity to a pitch of agony that he, with his equable disposition, could never know.

He was glad to get rid of them all, to see the last black-robed figure disappear, to hear the last word of sympathy which grated on his soul. He could not answer with canting phrases of would-be resignation. No ; if he had spoken at all, it must have been in the volume of curses, frozen in his heart.

Mary, with her apron to her eyes, was drawing up the blinds. She hurried away when her master came in, as if ashamed of being found in the act of doing away with the outward signs of mourning ; but, taking no notice of her, he sauntered to the window, with his hands in his pockets, and looked out. Presently, he walked into the garden. A man looked over the hedge and watched him, but he did not notice him.

The day wore on, rain began to fall, but still
he paced the lawn, backwards and forwards,
with a frown on his white face, and his hands
clasped behind him. The raindrops pattered
on the roses, the birds twittered under the eaves,
a little kitten came and stared at the solitary
black figure, which looked like a moving splash
of ink on the green grass. Mary laid the cloth,
watching her master furtively from the window,
as she arranged the spoons and forks. There
was something in the fixed expression of his
face, in the unvaried monotony of his walk,
which frightened her. When the dinner was
ready, she had scarcely the courage to tell him.

At the sound of her voice, as she announced
it timidly from under the shelter of the porch,
he stood still and turned his eyes upon her.
They looked as if they had stared, and stared, at
a thing of horror, till the horror was congealed
in their black depths, and the girl shivered.

"You can take it away," he said calmly, and
resumed his walk.

The evening shadows crept from the duskier
corners of the small garden and gathered round
him, as he paced up and down the patch of
soaking grass—alone, for ever alone with the
darkness of his thoughts. Who could fathom
the depths of his most undivine despair; gauge
the length and breadth of the misery which had

come stealthily after him, like the steps of the avenging deities, " shod with wool ; " come after him when his happiness was already in his grasp ; come after him like a creeping assassin, and killed the only thing in life which gave him joy ?

There was nothing left. The world, with all its broken promises, shattered at a blow, was empty—literally empty. Turn which way he would, was there anything to tempt him—anything to make him wish for length of days ; anything to make it possible to live on as he had done before, when there was the loveliest prize, that eye had ever seen, to be won by patience and the struggling efforts of man's endeavour ? Was it worth while to cherish that which had lost all value—to keep it when its possession meant a prolongation of such torment as Dante has given to the damned ?

His mind was a chaos, through which desperate thoughts darted like destructive comets, lurid with the glow of evil fires, borrowed from the spirits of darkness for man's despair. It was late when he went into the house, carrying these evil thoughts with him into the dining-room, where he poured out a tumblerful of wine—into his bedroom, where he threw himself down on his sleepless bed.

The next day, he resumed his usual routine of duty at the barracks. The colonel, seeing

him at the head of his company at the morning's
drill, and struck by his haggard face, told him
that he had better take a fortnight's extra leave;
but the kindly offer was declined with thanks.
His brother-officers, moved by compassion, came
up to shake hands with him, a ceremony which
they had dispensed with lately, on account of a
report which had spread through the regiment
that there was something decidedly shady in his
conduct with regard to the Tremayne affair;
but they found that Angus Balfour was not a
fellow to be dropped one day, and picked up the
next. With a chilly bow, he retired into himself,
and kept apart.

The cottage, with all its pretty new furniture,
was to be let to any stranger who would care to
take it; Benson and Mary were dismissed with
a month's wages, and told to go at once.

They were still lingering about the place, when
Balfour came in, unexpectedly, late in the afternoon. Walking straight through the house, he
fetched some wooden cases from an outbuilding,
and dragged them into the drawing-room.

"Bring all the things that belonged to your
mistress, and put them in here," he said sternly
to Mary.

She ran upstairs at once, and presently returned with an armful of pretty dresses, which
she laid carefully in one of the boxes, her own

tears falling fast, whilst his were dry. Never till her dying day will she forget that hour of incessant packing. Every little tiny knick-knack, which the dead bride had worn or cherished, was placed in one or other of the cases. All the while Balfour never spoke a word, pointing dumbly to the various articles which he wished her to hand to him. With his white face, his stern eyes, and his mute tongue, he made a creepy feeling go down her back, and her fingers shook so that a delicate blue vase slipped through them on to the floor. He looked at her—that was enough; worse than a hundred scoldings—and kicked the pieces aside. The cases were closed at last, and he fetched a hammer and some nails to fasten down their lids securely. When this was done, he passed a cord round each, wrote a label, directed to Mr. Ward, tied it on, and turned to Mary.

"See that these boxes are sent to the station," he said briefly; "and those books lying on the table must be returned to the library."

With a nod of dismissal, he left the room and went upstairs, as if to fetch something. When he came down he gave one look round at the desolation he had worked in the pretty room, and turned his back on the house, where he had known the acme of joy and the climax of sorrow. The two servants watched him as he walked down the road in his undress uniform, his sword clanking by his side; and their hearts were heavy with foreboding.

A man stepped out of the shelter of the hedge, and followed him at a little distance.

"If the master had but owed a penny in the place," remarked the cook, "I could have taken my 'davy that fellow was a bailiff."

"He has been hanging about for the last day or two," said Mary, nervously. "I hope he ain't a burglar looking out for a job."

Balfour, caring nothing as to whether he were dogged by a whole army of spies or not, walked on, looking neither to right nor left. A child, running after a kite, tripped up and fell down straight in front of him. The little thing looked up into his dark face, with its rosy mouth pursed up for a cry. Balfour pushed it on one side with his foot, and passed on. Down the road, with its fringe of cosy villas, each looking like a separate home of comfort and peace, through the town, still with eyes looking straight in front, and without a pause, on to the sweet fresh country beyond. A policeman came straight from the Bedford police-station, and joined the man in the rear, who pointed to the figure in front, and they both walked on together.

As if goaded by some inward impulse, Balfour

hurried on, utterly unconscious of the men
behind, or the pleasant green fields on either
side. There was fever in his brain, and ice in
his heart. Earth had no corner in which he
could hide his head and be still. He never
stopped until he reached the gate of the
cemetery, resting so peacefully on the quiet
hillside. Stepping quickly over the graves, he
sought out one, where the newly turned sods
showed that she who rested beneath their kindly
covering had been but recently laid to her rest.

His face was stern and rigid as ever as he
stood by his wife's grave. Wild and lawless in
grief or joy, he could not bend his stubborn
spirit to any pretence of resignation. He could
not let his Kate go from him without crying
out—however futile the cry—against the injustice of Heaven, which took his one ewe lamb
from him, and left a fold of sheep to others on
either side. To win her, he had bartered his
own self-respect, his place amongst honourable
men, his chances of promotion in his profession,
and the affection of the only man in the world
who was willing out of pure love to stand by his
side as a friend. And all he had gained in
return was a grave, where every earthly hope
and desire lay buried, and the prospect of a
convict's cell!

He stood like a statue, looking down on the

grass with hungry eyes, as if he fain would
pierce to the lovely form below and clasp it
once more to his desolate heart. Would death
unite, or divide? The question kept repeating
itself in his tortured brain. Would their two
spirits cleave to each other in the realms of
shadow, and live over again the love and the
rapture of the past few months? If that were
possible, death would be indeed more welcome
than water to the driven-mad-with-thirst. But
if retribution must follow the sinner beyond the
grave—if Kate's pure spirit were raised to a
heaven of bliss, and his guilty soul consigned to
a Hades further apart than the poles—then
death would only add one torment to another in
a long continuous chain.

He raised his yearning eyes to the sky, now
red with the glory and brightness of the setting
sun, as if he would wring an answer from its
passing clouds.

> "Is there never a chink in the word above,
> Where they listen to words from below?"

His heart was in a tumult—wild irrepressible
longing for what could never be again, wild
tempestuous revolt against the hardness of his
fate. Tremayne had never suffered like this,
even when he stood in the felon's dock, with the
stain of its shame upon him. He had never

staked honour and happiness on the cast of a
die, and known what it was to lose them.

Slowly the minutes passed. Afraid to live,
and yet loth to die with his question unsolved.
Earthly love so entirely possessed his soul, that
his only fear as to that dim unchangeable future,
beyond the limits of mortal men, was, lest it
should mean for him separation from his bride!

Driven out of himself by the strength of his
desire, he stretched out his arms to the silent
mound, as if it could answer back. "Kate," he
cried in a hoarse whisper, "shall we be together
if I come?" and then stood still, and waited.
No sound but a sudden gust of wind, which
played with the flowers cast by loving hands on
a neighbouring grave. A little spray of jessamine,
whirled from its resting-place, fell at his feet.
Jessamine was Kate's favourite flower, and to
her husband it seemed like her answer from the
land "that is very far off." "I come," he said
softly, as he picked it up and kissed it.

The policemen had halted at the gate; not
yet turned into wooden machines by the harden-
ing practice of their profession, they felt some
compassion for the widower, whom it was their
duty to arrest, and they thought they would
leave him a little space for the indulgence of a
silent tear. They were in such a position that
they could keep him in sight, without being

seen. Tired of waiting, they had just made up their minds that further delay was unadvisable, when, sharp and shrill, a pistol-shot rang through the air. Then, cursing their own stupidity, they rushed to the spot.

Balfour was lying face downwards on his wife's grave, shot through the heart. Turning him over gently, they saw at a glance that they were too late. The rays of the setting sun fell slantwise across the handsome features, calm and peaceful in the sudden stillness of death, with no outward sign on their impassive beauty of the trouble and despair of his last moments.

Afraid to face the consequences of his sins on earth, he had rushed into the presence of the Judge on high, with no repentance for the past in his stormy heart, no prayer for the unknown future on his scornful lips.

THE END.

LONDON: PRINTED BY WILLIAM CLOWES AND SONS, LIMITED, STAMFORD STREET AND CHARING CROSS.

A Catalogue of American and Foreign Books Published or Imported by MESSRS. SAMPSON LOW & CO. *can be had on application.*

Crown Buildings, 188, *Fleet Street, London,*
November, 1882.

𝕬 𝕾𝖊𝖑𝖊𝖈𝖙𝖎𝖔𝖓 𝖋𝖗𝖔𝖒 𝖙𝖍𝖊 𝕷𝖎𝖘𝖙 𝖔𝖋 𝕭𝖔𝖔𝖐𝖘

PUBLISHED BY

SAMPSON LOW, MARSTON, SEARLE, & RIVINGTON.

ALPHABETICAL LIST.

A CLASSIFIED *Educational Catalogue of Works* published in Great Britain. Demy 8vo, cloth extra. Second Edition, revised and corrected, 5*s*.

About Some Fellows. By an ETON BOY, Author of "A Day of my Life." Cloth limp, square 16mo, 2*s* 6*d*.

Adams (C. K.) Manual of Historical Literature. Crown 8vo, 12*s*. 6*d*.

Adventures of a Young Naturalist. By LUCIEN BIART, with 117 beautiful Illustrations on Wood. Edited and adapted by PARKER GILLMORE. Post 8vo, cloth extra, gilt edges, New Edition, 7*s*. 6*d*.

Alcott (Louisa M.) Jimmy's Cruise in the " Pinafore." With 9 Illustrations. Second Edition. Small post 8vo, cloth gilt, 3*s*. 6*d*.

—— *Aunt Jo's Scrap-Bag.* Square 16mo, 2*s*. 6*d*. (Rose Library, 1*s*.)

—— *Little Men : Life at Plumfield with Jo's Boys.* Small post 8vo, cloth, gilt edges, 3*s*. 6*d*. (Rose Library, Double vol. 2*s*.)

—— *Little Women.* 1 vol., cloth, gilt edges, 3*s*. 6*d*. (Rose Library, 2 vols., 1*s*. each.)

—— *Old-Fashioned Girl.* Best Edition, small post 8vo, cloth extra, gilt edges, 3*s*. 6*d*. (Rose Library, 2*s*.)

—— *Work, and Beginning Again.* A Story of Experience. (Rose Library, 2 vols., 1*s*. each.)

—— *Shawl Straps.* Small post 8vo, cloth extra, gilt, 3*s*. 6*d*.

—— *Eight Cousins ; or, the Aunt Hill.* Small post 8vo, with Illustrations, 3*s*. 6*d*.

—— *The Rose in Bloom.* Small post 8vo, 3*s*. 6*d*.

—— *Under the Lilacs.* Small post 8vo, cloth extra, 5*s*.

A

Alcott (Louisa M.) An Old-Fashioned Thanksgiving Day. Small post 8vo, 3s. 6d.

—— *Proverbs.* Small post 8vo, 3s. 6d.

—— *Jack and Jill.* Small post 8vo, cloth extra, 5s.
"Miss Alcott's stories are thoroughly healthy, full of racy fun and humour . . . exceedingly entertaining . . . . We can recommend the 'Eight Cousins.'"—*Athenæum.*

Aldrich (T. B.) Friar Jerome's Beautiful Book, &c. Very choicely printed on hand-made paper, parchment cover, 3s. 6d.

—— *Poetical Works. Édition de Luxe.* Very handsomely bound and illustrated, 21s.

Alford (Lady Marian) See "Embroidery."

Allen (E. A.) Rock me to Sleep, Mother. 18 full-page Illustrations, elegantly bound, fcap. 4to, 5s.

American Men of Letters. Lives of Thoreau, Irving, Webster. Small post 8vo, cloth, 2s. 6d. each.

Ancient Greek Female Costume. By J. MOYR SMITH. Crown 8vo, 112 full-page Plates and other Illustrations, 7s. 6d.

Andersen (Hans Christian) Fairy Tales. With 10 full-page Illustrations in Colours by E. V. B. Cheap Edition, 5s.

Andres (E.) Fabrication of Volatile and Fat Varnishes, Lacquers, Siccatives, and Sealing Waxes. 8vo, 12s. 6d.

Angling Literature in England; and Descriptions of Fishing by the Ancients. By O. LAMBERT. With a Notice of some Books on other Piscatorial Subjects. Fcap. 8vo, vellum, top gilt, 3s. 6d.

Archer (William) English Dramatists of To-day. Crown 8vo, 8s. 6d.

Arnold (G. M.) Robert Pocock, the Gravesend Historian. Crown 8vo, cloth. [*In the Press.*

Art and Archæology (Dictionary). See "Illustrated."

Art Education. See "Illustrated Text Books," "Illustrated Dictionary," "Biographies of Great Artists."

Art Workmanship in Gold and Silver. Large 8vo, 2s. 6d.

Art Workmanship in Porcelain. Large 8vo, 2s. 6d.

Artists, Great. See "Biographies."

Audsley (G. A.) Ornamental Arts of Japan. 90 Plates, 74 in Colours and Gold, with General and Descriptive Text. 2 vols., folio, £16 16s.

Audsley (W. and G. A.) Outlines of Ornament. Small folio, very numerous Illustrations, 31s. 6d.

Auerbach (B.) Spinoza. 2 vols., 18mo, 4s.

Autumnal Leaves. By F. G. HEATH. Illustrated by 12 Plates, exquisitely coloured after Nature; 4 Page and 14 Vignette Drawings. Cloth, imperial 16mo, gilt edges, 14*s.*

BANCROFT (*G.*) *History of the Constitution of the United* States of America. 2 vols., 8vo, 24*s.*

Barrett. English Church Composers. Crown 8vo, 3*s.*

THE BAYARD SERIES.

Edited by the late J. HAIN FRISWELL.

Comprising Pleasure Books of Literature produced in the Choicest Style as Companionable Volumes at Home and Abroad.

"We can hardly imagine better books for boys to read or for men to ponder over."—*Times.*

Price 2s. 6d. each Volume, complete in itself, flexible cloth extra, gilt edges, with silk Headbands and Registers.

The Story of the Chevalier Bayard. By M. De Berville.

De Joinville's St. Louis, King of France.

The Essays of Abraham Cowley, including all his Prose Works.

Abdallah; or, The Four Leaves. By Edouard Laboullaye.

Table-Talk and Opinions of Napoleon Buonaparte.

Vathek: An Oriental Romance. By William Beckford.

The King and the Commons. A Selection of Cavalier and Puritan Songs. Edited by Professor Morley.

Words of Wellington: Maxims and Opinions of the Great Duke.

Dr. Johnson's Rasselas, Prince of Abyssinia. With Notes.

Hazlitt's Round Table. With Biographical Introduction.

The Religio Medici, Hydriotaphia, and the Letter to a Friend. By Sir Thomas Browne, Knt.

Ballad Poetry of the Affections. By Robert Buchanan.

Coleridge's Christabel, and other Imaginative Poems. With Preface by Algernon C. Swinburne.

Lord Chesterfield's Letters, Sentences, and Maxims. With Introduction by the Editor, and Essay on Chesterfield by M. de Ste.-Beuve, of the French Academy.

Essays in Mosaic. By Thos. Ballantyne.

My Uncle Toby; his Story and his Friends. Edited by P. Fitzgerald.

Reflections; or, Moral Sentences and Maxims of the Duke de la Rochefoucauld.

Socrates: Memoirs for English Readers from Xenophon's Memorabilia. By Edw. Levien.

Prince Albert's Golden Precepts.

A Case containing 12 Volumes, price 31s. 6d.; or the Case separately, price 3s. 6d.

Beaconsfield (*Life of Lord*). See "Hitchman."

Begum's Fortune (*The*): *A New Story.* By JULES VERNE. Translated by W. H. G. KINGSTON. Numerous Illustrations. Crown 8vo, cloth, gilt edges, 7*s.* 6*d.*; plainer binding, plain edges, 5*s.*

A 2

Ben Hur: A Tale of the Christ. By L. WALLACE. Crown 8vo, 6s.

Beumers' German Copybooks. In six gradations at 4d. each.

Bickersteth's Hymnal Companion to Book of Common Prayer may be had in various styles and bindings from 1d. to 21s. *Price List and Prospectus will be forwarded on application.*

Bickersteth (Rev. E. H., M.A.) The Clergyman in his Home. Small post 8vo, 1s.

—— *The Master's Home-Call; or, Brief Memorials of Alice* Frances Bickersteth. 20th Thousand. 32mo, cloth gilt, 1s.

—— *The Master's Will.* A Funeral Sermon preached on the Death of Mrs. S. Gurney Buxton. Sewn, 6d.; cloth gilt, 1s.

—— *The Shadow of the Rock.* A Selection of Religious Poetry. 18mo, cloth extra, 2s. 6d.

—— *The Shadowed Home and the Light Beyond.* 7th Edition, crown 8vo, cloth extra, 5s.

Biographies of the Great Artists (Illustrated). Crown 8vo, emblematical binding, 3s. 6d. per volume, except where the price is given.

Claude Lorrain.*	Mantegna and Francia.
Correggio, by M. E. Heaton, 2s. 6d.	Meissonier, by J. W. Mollett, 2s. 6d.
Della Robbia and Cellini, 2s. 6d.*	Michelangelo Buonarotti, by Clément.
Albrecht Dürer, by R. F. Heath.	Murillo, by Ellen E. Minor, 2s. 6d.
Figure Painters of Holland.	Overbeck, by J. B. Atkinson.
Fra Angelico, Masaccio, and Botticelli.	Raphael, by N. D'Anvers.
Fra Bartolommeo, Albertinelli, and	Rembrandt, by J. W. Mollett.
Andrea del Sarto.	Reynolds, by F. S. Pulling.
Gainsborough and Constable.	Rubens, by C. W. Kett.
Ghiberti and Donatello, 2s. 6d.	Tintoretto, by W. R. Osler.
Giotto, by Harry Quilter.	Titian, by R. F. Heath.
Hans Holbein, by Joseph Cundall.	Turner, by Cosmo Monkhouse.
Hogarth, by Austin Dobson.	Vandyck and Hals, by P. R. Head.
Landseer, by F. G. Stevens.	Velasquez, by E. Stowe.
Lawrence and Romney, by Lord	Vernet and Delaroche, by J. R.
Ronald Gower, 2s. 6d.	Rees.
Leonardo da Vinci.	Watteau, by J. W. Mollett, 2s. 6d.*
Little Masters of Germany, by W.	Wilkie, by J. W. Mollett.
B. Scott.	

* *Not yet published.*

Bird (H. E.) Chess Practice. 8vo, 2s. 6d.

Birthday Book. Extracts from the Writings of R. W. Emerson. Square 16mo, cloth extra, numerous Illustrations, very choice binding, 3s. 6d.

—— *Extracts from the Poems of Whittier.* Square 16mo, with numerous Illustrations and handsome binding, 3s. 6d.

Birthday Book. Extracts from the Writings of Thomas à Kempis. Large 16mo, red lines, 3s. 6d.

Black (Wm.) Three Feathers. Small post 8vo, cloth extra, 6s.

—— *Lady Silverdale's Sweetheart, and other Stories.* 1 vol., small post 8vo, 6s.

—— *Kilmeny: a Novel.* Small post 8vo, cloth, 6s.

—— *In Silk Attire.* 3rd Edition, small post 8vo, 6s.

—— *A Daughter of Heth.* 11th Edition, small post 8vo, 6s.

—— *Sunrise.* Small post 8vo, 6s.

Blackmore (R. D.) Lorna Doone. Small post 8vo, 6s.

—— *Edition de luxe.* Crown 4to, very numerous Illustrations, cloth, gilt edges, 31s. 6d.; parchment, uncut, top gilt, 35s.

—— *Alice Lorraine.* Small post 8vo, 6s.

—— *Clara Vaughan.* 6s.

—— *Cradock Nowell.* New Edition, 6s.

—— *Cripps the Carrier.* 3rd Edition, small post 8vo, 6s.

—— *Mary Anerley.* New Edition, small post 8vo, 6s.

—— *Erema ; or, My Father's Sin.* Small post 8vo, 6s.

—— *Christowell.* Small post 8vo, 6s.

Blossoms from the King's Garden : Sermons for Children. By the Rev. C. BOSANQUET. 2nd Edition, small post 8vo, cloth extra, 6s.

Bock (Carl). The Head Hunters of Borneo : Up the Mahakkam, and Down the Barita; also Journeyings in Sumatra. 1 vol., super-royal 8vo, 32 Coloured Plates, cloth extra, 36s.

Bonwick (James) First Twenty Years of Australia. Crown 8vo, 5s.

—— *Port Philip Settlement.* 8vo, numerous Illustrations, 21s.

Book of the Play. By DUTTON COOK. New and Revised Edition. 1 vol., cloth extra, 3s. 6d.

Bower (G. S.) Law relating to Electric Lighting. Crown 8vo, 5s.

Boy's Froissart (The). Selected from the Chronicles of England, France, and Spain. Illustrated, square crown 8vo, 7s. 6d. See "Froissart."

Boy's King Arthur (The). With very fine Illustrations. Square crown 8vo, cloth extra, gilt edges, 7s. 6d. Edited by SIDNEY LANIER, Editor of "The Boy's Froissart."

Boy's Mabinogion (The) : being the Original Welsh Legends of King Arthur. Edited by SIDNEY LANIER. With numerous very graphic Illustrations. Crown 8vo, cloth, gilt edges, 7s. 6d.

Brassey (Lady) Tahiti. With Photos. by Colonel Stuart-Wortley. Fcap. 4to, 21s.

Breton Folk: An Artistic Tour in Brittany. By HENRY BLACKBURN, Author of "Artists and Arabs," "Normandy Picturesque," &c. With 171 Illustrations by RANDOLPH CALDECOTT. Imperial 8vo, cloth extra, gilt edges, 21s.; plainer binding, 10s. 6d.

Bryant (W. C.) and Gay (S. H.) History of the United States. 4 vols., royal 8vo, profusely Illustrated, 60s.

Bryce (Prof.) Manitoba. Crown 8vo, 7s. 6d.

Burnaby (Capt.). See "On Horseback."

Burnham Beeches (Heath, F. G.). With numerous Illustrations and a Map. Crown 8vo, cloth, gilt edges, 3s. 6d. Second Edition.

Butler (W. F.) The Great Lone Land; an Account of the Red River Expedition, 1869-70. With Illustrations and Map. Fifth and Cheaper Edition, crown 8vo, cloth extra, 7s. 6d.

————— *Invasion of England, told twenty years after, by an Old* Soldier. Crown 8vo, 2s. 6d.

————— *The Wild North Land; the Story of a Winter Journey* with Dogs across Northern North America. Demy 8vo, cloth, with numerous Woodcuts and a Map, 4th Edition, 18s. Cr. 8vo, 7s. 6d.

————— *Red Cloud; or, the Solitary Sioux.* Imperial 16mo, numerous illustrations, gilt edges, 7s. 6d.

Buxton (H. J. W.) Painting, English and American. Crown 8vo, 5s.

CADOGAN (Lady A.) Illustrated Games of Patience. Twenty-four Diagrams in Colours, with Descriptive Text. Foolscap 4to, cloth extra, gilt edges, 3rd Edition, 12s. 6d.

California. Illustrated, 12s. 6d. See "Nordhoff."

Cambridge Trifles; or, Splutterings from an Undergraduate Pen. By the Author of "A Day of my Life at Eton," &c. 16mo, cloth extra, 2s. 6d.

Capello (H.) and Ivens (R.) From Benguella to the Territory of Yacca. Translated by ALFRED ELWES. With Maps and over 130 full-page and text Engravings. 2 vols., 8vo, 42s.

Carlyle (T.) Reminiscences of my Irish Journey in 1849. Crown 8vo, 7s. 6d.

Challamel (M. A.) History of Fashion in France. With 21 Plates, specially coloured by hand, satin-wood binding, imperial 8vo, 28s.

Changed Cross (The), and other Religious Poems. 16mo, 2s. 6d.

Child of the Cavern (The); or, Strange Doings Underground. By JULES VERNE. Translated by W. H. G. KINGSTON. Numerous Illustrations. Sq. cr. 8vo, gilt edges, 7s. 6d.; cl., plain edges, 3s. 6d.

Choice Editions of Choice Books. 2*s.* 6*d.* each. Illustrated by
C. W. COPE, R.A., T. CRESWICK, R.A., E. DUNCAN, BIRKET
FOSTER, J. C. HORSLEY, A.R.A., G. HICKS, R. REDGRAVE, R.A.,
C. STONEHOUSE, F. TAYLER, G. THOMAS, H. J. TOWNSHEND,
E. H. WEHNERT, HARRISON WEIR, &c.

Bloomfield's Farmer's Boy.	Milton's L'Allegro.
Campbell's Pleasures of Hope.	Poetry of Nature. Harrison Weir.
Coleridge's Ancient Mariner.	Rogers' (Sam.) Pleasures of Memory.
Goldsmith's Deserted Village.	Shakespeare's Songs and Sonnets.
Goldsmith's Vicar of Wakefield.	Tennyson's May Queen.
Gray's Elegy in a Churchyard.	Elizabethan Poets.
Keat's Eve of St. Agnes.	Wordsworth's Pastoral Poems.

" Such works are a glorious beatification for a poet."—*Athenæum.*

Christ in Song. By Dr. PHILIP SCHAFF. A New Edition,
revised, cloth, gilt edges, 6*s.*

Confessions of a Frivolous Girl (The) : A Novel of Fashionable
Life. Edited by ROBERT GRANT. Crown 8vo, 6*s.* Paper boards, 1*s.*

Coote (W.) Wanderings South by East. Illustrated, 8vo, 21*s.*

Cornet of Horse (The) : A Story for Boys. By G. A. HENTY.
Crown 8vo, cloth extra, gilt edges, numerous graphic Illustrations, 5*s.*

Cripps the Carrier. 3rd Edition, 6*s.* *See* BLACKMORE.

Cruise of H.M.S. " Challenger" (The). By W. J. J. SPRY, R.N.
With Route Map and many Illustrations. 6th Edition, demy 8vo, cloth,
18*s.* Cheap Edition, crown 8vo, some of the Illustrations, 7*s.* 6*d.*

Cruise of the Walnut Shell (The). An instructive and amusing
Story, told in Rhyme, for Children. With 32 Coloured Plates.
Square fancy boards, 5*s.*

D'ANVERS (N.) An Elementary History of Art. Crown
8vo, 10*s.* 6*d.*

—— *Elementary History of Music.* Crown 8vo, 2*s.* 6*d.*

Daughter (A) of Heth. By W. BLACK. Crown 8vo, 6*s.*

Day of My Life (A) ; or, Every-Day Experiences at Eton.
By an ETON BOY, Author of "About Some Fellows." 16mo, cloth
extra, 2*s.* 6*d.* 6th Thousand.

Decoration. Vol. II., folio, 6*s.* Vol. III., New Series, folio,
7*s.* 6*d.*

De Leon (E.) Egypt under its Khedives. With Map and
Illustrations. Crown 8vo, 4*s.*

Dick Cheveley : his Fortunes and Misfortunes. By W. H. G.
KINGSTON. 350 pp., square 16mo, and 22 full-page Illustrations.
Cloth, gilt edges, 7*s.* 6*d.* ; plainer binding, plain edges, 5*s.*

Dick Sands, the Boy Captain. By JULES VERNE. With nearly
100 Illustrations, cloth, gilt, 10s. 6d.; plain binding and plain edges, 5s.

Don Quixote, Wit and Wisdom of. By EMMA THOMPSON.
Square fcap. 8vo, 3s. 6d.

Donnelly (F.) Atlantis in the Antediluvian World. Crown
8vo, 12s. 6d.

Dos Passos (F. R.) Law of Stockbrokers and Stock Exchanges.
8vo, 35s.

*E*GYPT. See "Senior," "De Leon," "Foreign Countries."

Eight Cousins. *See* ALCOTT.

Electric Lighting. A Comprehensive Treatise. By J. E. H.
GORDON. 8vo, fully Illustrated.   [*In preparation.*

Elementary History (An) of Art. Comprising Architecture,
Sculpture, Painting, and the Applied Arts. By N. D'ANVERS.
With a Preface by Professor ROGER SMITH. New Edition, illustrated
with upwards of 200 Wood Engravings. Crown 8vo, strongly bound
in cloth, price 10s. 6d.

Elementary History (An) of Music. Edited by OWEN J.
DULLEA. Illustrated with Portraits of the most eminent Composers,
and Engravings of the Musical Instruments of many Nations. Crown
8vo, cloth, 2s. 6d.

Elinor Dryden. By Mrs. MACQUOID. Crown 8vo, 6s.

Embroidery (Handbook of). Edited by LADY MARIAN ALFORD,
and published by authority of the Royal School of Art Needlework.
With 22 Coloured Plates, Designs, &c. Crown 8vo, 5s.

Emerson (R. W.) Life and Writings. Crown 8vo, 8s. 6d.

English Catalogue of Books. Vol. III., 1872—1880. Royal
8vo, half-morocco, 42s.

———— *Dramatists of To-day.* By W. ARCHER, M.A. Crown
8vo, 8s. 6d.

English Philosophers. Edited by E. B. IVAN MÜLLER, M.A.

A series intended to give a concise view of the works and lives of English
thinkers. Crown 8vo volumes of 180 or 200 pp., price 3s. 6d. each.

Francis Bacon, by Thomas Fowler.	*John Stuart Mill, by Miss Helen
Hamilton, by W. H. S. Monck.	Taylor.
Hartley and James Mill, by G. S.	Shaftesbury and Hutcheson, by
Bower.	Professor Fowler.
	Adam Smith, by J. A. Farrer.

* *Not yet published.*

Episodes in the Life of an Indian Chaplain. Crown 8vo,
cloth extra, 12s. 6d.

Episodes of French History. Edited, with Notes, Maps, and Illustrations, by GUSTAVE MASSON, B.A. Small 8vo, 2s. 6d. each.
    1. **Charlemagne and the Carlovingians.**
    2. **Louis XI. and the Crusades.**
    3. **Part I. Francis I. and Charles V.**
      ,, **II. Francis I. and the Renaissance.**
    4. **Henry IV. and the End of the Wars of Religion.**

Erema ; or, My Father's Sin. 6s. *See* BLACKMORE.

Etcher (*The*). Containing 36 Examples of the Original Etched-work of Celebrated Artists, amongst others : BIRKET FOSTER, J. E. HODGSON, R.A., COLIN HUNTER, J. P. HESELTINE, ROBERT W. MACBETH, R. S. CHATTOCK, &c. Vols. for 1881 and 1882, imperial 4to, cloth extra, gilt edges, 2l. 12s. 6d. each.

Eton. *See* "Day of my Life," "Out of School," "About Some Fellows."

*F*ARM *Ballads.* By WILL CARLETON. Boards, 1s. ; cloth, gilt edges, 1s. 6d.

Farm Festivals. By the same Author. Uniform with above.

Farm Legends. By the same Author. See above.

Fashion (*History of*). See "Challamel."

Fechner (*G. T.*) *On Life after Death.* 12mo, vellum, 2s. 6d.

Felkin (*R. W.*) *and Wilson* (*Rev. C. T.*) *Uganda and the* Egyptian Soudan. An Account of Travel in Eastern and Equatorial Africa ; including a Residence of Two Years at the Court of King Mtesa, and a Description of the Slave Districts of Bahr-el-Ghazel and Darfour. With a New Map of 1200 miles in these Provinces ; numerous Illustrations, and Notes. By R. W. FELKIN, F.R.G.S., &c., &c. ; and the Rev. C. T. WILSON, M.A. Oxon., F.R.G.S. 2 vols., crown 8vo, cloth, 28s.

Fern Paradise (*The*) : *A Plea for the Culture of Ferns.* By F. G. HEATH. New Edition, fully Illustrated, large post 8vo, cloth, gilt edges, 12s. 6d. Sixth Edition.

Fern World (*The*). By F. G. HEATH. Illustrated by Twelve Coloured Plates, giving complete Figures (Sixty-four in all) of every Species of British Fern, printed from Nature ; by several full-page and other Engravings. Cloth, gilt edges, 6th Edition, 12s. 6d.

Few Hints on Proving Wills (*A*). Enlarged Edition, 1s.

Fields (*J. T.*) *Yesterdays with Authors.* New Ed., 8vo., 16s.

First Steps in Conversational French Grammar. By F. JULIEN.
Being an Introduction to "Petites Leçons de Conversation et de
Grammaire," by the same Author. Fcap. 8vo, 128 pp., 1*s.*

Florence. See "Yriarte."

Flowers of Shakespeare. 32 beautifully Coloured Plates. 5*s.*

Four Lectures on Electric Induction. Delivered at the Royal
Institution, 1878-9. By J. E. H. GORDON, B.A. Cantab. With
numerous Illustrations. Cloth limp, square 16mo, 3*s.*

Foreign Countries and British Colonies. A series of Descriptive
Handbooks. Each volume will be the work of a writer who has
special acquaintance with the subject. Crown 8vo, 3*s.* 6*d.* each.

Australia, by J. F. Vesey Fitzgerald.	Peru, by Clements R. Markham,
Austria, by D. Kay, F.R.G.S.	C.B.
*Canada, by W. Fraser Rae.	Russia, by W. R. Morfill, M.A.
Denmark and Iceland, by E. C.	Spain, by Rev. Wentworth Webster.
Otté.	Sweden and Norway, by F. H.
Egypt, by S. Lane Poole, B.A.	Woods.
France, by Miss M. Roberts.	*Switzerland, by W. A. P. Coolidg
Greece, by L. Sergeant, B.A.	M.A.
*Holland, by R. L. Poole.	*Turkey-in-Asia, by J. C. McCoan,
Japan, by S. Mossman.	M.P.
*New Zealand.	West Indies, by C. H. Eden,
*Persia, by Major-Gen. Sir F. Gold-	F.R.G.S.
smid.	

* Not ready yet.

Franc (Maud Jeanne). The following form one Series, small
post 8vo, in uniform cloth bindings, with gilt edges:—

Emily's Choice. 5*s.*	Vermont Vale. 5*s.*
Hall's Vineyard. 4*s.*	Minnie's Mission. 4*s.*
John's Wife: A Story of Life in	Little Mercy. 5*s.*
South Australia. 4*s.*	Beatrice Melton's Discipline. 4*s.*
Marian; or, The Light of Some	No Longer a Child. 4*s.*
One's Home. 5*s.*	Golden Gifts. 5*s.*
Silken Cords and Iron Fetters. 4*s.*	Two Sides to Every Question. 5*s.*

Francis (F.) War, Waves, and Wanderings, including a Cruise
in the "Lancashire Witch." 2 vols., crown 8vo, cloth extra, 24*s.*

Froissart (The Boy's). Selected from the Chronicles of England, France, Spain, &c. By SIDNEY LANIER. The Volume is
fully Illustrated, and uniform with "The Boy's King Arthur." Crown
8vo, cloth, 7*s.* 6*d.*

From Newfoundland to Manitoba; a Guide through Canada's
Maritime, Mining, and Prairie Provinces. By W. FRASER RAE.
Crown 8vo, with several Maps, 6*s.*

G*AMES of Patience.* *See* CADOGAN.

Gentle Life (Queen Edition). 2 vols. in 1, small 4to, 6s.

THE GENTLE LIFE SERIES.

Price 6s. each ; or in calf extra, price 10s. 6d. ; Smaller Edition, cloth extra, 2s. 6d.

The Gentle Life. Essays in aid of the Formation of Character of Gentlemen and Gentlewomen.

About in the World. Essays by Author of " The Gentle Life."

Like unto Christ. A New Translation of Thomas à Kempis' " De Imitatione Christi."

Familiar Words. An Index Verborum, or Quotation Handbook. 6s.

Essays by Montaigne. Edited and Annotated by the Author of "The Gentle Life."

The Gentle Life. 2nd Series.

The Silent Hour: Essays, Original and Selected. By the Author of "The Gentle Life."

Half-Length Portraits. Short Studies of Notable Persons. By J. HAIN FRISWELL.

Essays on English Writers, for the Self-improvement of Students in English Literature.

Other People's Windows. By J. HAIN FRISWELL.

A Man's Thoughts. By J. HAIN FRISWELL.

Gilder (W. H.) Schwatka's Search. Sledging in quest of the Franklin Records. Illustrated, 8vo, 12s. 6d.

Gilpin's Forest Scenery. Edited by F. G. HEATH. Large post 8vo, with numerous Illustrations. Uniform with "The Fern World," re-issued, 7s. 6d.

Gordon (J. E. H.). See "Four Lectures on Electric Induction," "Physical Treatise on Electricity," "Electric Lighting."

Gouffé. The Royal Cookery Book. By JULES GOUFFÉ; translated and adapted for English use by ALPHONSE GOUFFÉ, Head Pastrycook to her Majesty the Queen. Illustrated with large plates printed in colours. 161 Woodcuts, 8vo, cloth extra, gilt edges, 2l. 2s.

—— Domestic Edition, half-bound, 10s. 6d.

"By far the ablest and most complete work on cookery that has ever been submitted to the gastronomical world."—*Pall Mall Gazette.*

Great Artists. See "Biographies."

Great Historic Galleries of England (The). Edited by LORD RONALD GOWER, F.S.A., Trustee of the National Portrait Gallery. Illustrated by 24 large and carefully executed *permanent* Photographs of some of the most celebrated Pictures by the Great Masters. Vol. I., imperial 4to, cloth extra, gilt edges, 36s. Vol. II., with 36 large permanent photographs, 2l. 12s. 6d.

Great Musicians. Edited by F. HUEFFER. A Series of Biographies, crown 8vo, 3s. each :—

Bach.	*Handel.	Schubert.
*Beethoven.	*Mendelssohn.	*Schumann.
*Berlioz.	*Mozart.	Richard Wagner.
English Church Composers.	Purcell.	Weber.
	Rossini.	

* *In preparation.*

Green (N.) A Thousand Years Hence. Crown 8vo, 6s.

Grohmann (W. A. B.) Camps in the Rockies. 8vo, 12s. 6d.

Guizot's History of France. Translated by ROBERT BLACK. Super-royal 8vo, very numerous Full-page and other Illustrations. In 8 vols., cloth extra, gilt, each 24s. This work is re-issued in cheaper binding, 8 vols., at 10s. 6d. each.

"It supplies a want which has long been felt, and ought to be in the hands of all students of history."—*Times.*

———————————————— *Masson's School Edition.* The History of France from the Earliest Times to the Outbreak of the Revolution ; abridged from the Translation by Robert Black, M.A., with Chronological Index, Historical and Genealogical Tables, &c. By Professor GUSTAVE MASSON, B.A., Assistant Master at Harrow School. With 24 full-page Portraits, and many other Illustrations. 1 vol., demy 8vo, 600 pp., cloth extra, 10s. 6d.

Guizot's History of England. In 3 vols. of about 500 pp. each, containing 60 to 70 Full-page and other Illustrations, cloth extra, gilt, 24s. each ; re-issue in cheaper binding, 10s. 6d. each.

"For luxury of typography, plainness of print, and beauty of illustration, these volumes, of which but one has as yet appeared in English, will hold their own against any production of an age so luxurious as our own in everything, typography not excepted."—*Times.*

Guyon (Mde.) Life. By UPHAM. 6th Edition, crown 8vo, 6s.

HANDBOOK to the Charities of London. See LOW'S.

Hall (W. W.) How to Live Long; or, 1408 Health Maxims, Physical, Mental, and Moral. By W. W. HALL, A.M., M.D. Small post 8vo, cloth, 2s. 2nd Edition.

Harper's Monthly Magazine. Published Monthly. 160 pages, fully Illustrated. 1s.

    Vol. I. December, 1880, to May, 1881.
    ,, II. May, 1881, to November, 1881.
    ,, III. June to November, 1882.

Super-royal 8vo, 8s. 6d. each.

    " 'Harper's Magazine' is so thickly sown with excellent illustrations that to count them would be a work of time ; not that it is a picture magazine, for the engravings illustrate the text after the manner seen in some of our choicest *éditions de luxe.*"—*St. James's Gazette.*

    "It is so pretty, so big, and so cheap. . . . An extraordinary shillingsworth—160 large octavo pages, with over a score of articles, and more than three times as many illustrations."—*Edinburgh Daily Review.*

    "An amazing shillingsworth . . . combining choice literature of both nations. '—*Nonconformist.*

*Hatton (Joseph) Journalistic London : Portraits and En-*gravings, with letterpress, of Distinguished Writers of the Day. Fcap. 4to, 12s. 6d.

———— *Three Recruits, and the Girls they left behind them.* Small post, 8vo, 6s.

    " It hurries us along in unflagging excitement."—*Times.*

Heart of Africa. Three Years' Travels and Adventures in the Unexplored Regions of Central Africa, from 1868 to 1871. By Dr. GEORG SCHWEINFURTH. Numerous Illustrations, and large Map. 2 vols., crown 8vo, cloth, 15s.

Heath (Francis George). *See* "Autumnal Leaves," "Burnham Beeches," "Fern Paradise," "Fern World," "Gilpin's Forest Scenery," "Our Woodland Trees," "Peasant Life," "Sylvan Spring," "Trees and Ferns," "Where to Find Ferns."

Heber's (Bishop) Illustrated Edition of Hymns. With upwards of 100 beautiful Engravings. Small 4to, handsomely bound, 7s. 6d. Morocco, 18s. 6d. and 21s. New and Cheaper Edition, cloth, 3s. 6d.

Heir of Kilfinnan (The). By W. H. G. KINGSTON. With Illustrations. Cloth, gilt edges, 7s. 6d. ; plainer binding, plain edges, 5s.

Heldmann (Bernard) Mutiny on Board the Ship "Leander." Small post 8vo, gilt edges, numerous Illustrations, 7s. 6d.

Henty (G. A.) Winning his Spurs. Numerous Illustrations. Crown 8vo, 5s.

———— *Cornet of Horse ;* which see.

Herrick (Robert) Poetry. Preface by AUSTIN DOBSON. With numerous Illustrations, by E. A. ABBEY. 4to, gilt edges, 42s.

History of a Crime (The) ; Deposition of an Eye-witness. The Story of the Coup d'État. By VICTOR HUGO. Crown 8vo, 6s.

History of Ancient Art. Translated from the German of JOHN WINCKELMANN, by JOHN LODGE, M.D. With very numerous Plates and Illustrations. 2 vols., 8vo, 36*s.*

—— *England. See* GUIZOT.

—— *English Literature. See* SCHERR.

—— *Fashion.* Coloured Plates. 28*s. See* CHALLAMEL.

—— *France. See* GUIZOT.

—— *Russia. See* RAMBAUD.

——·—— *Merchant Shipping. See* LINDSAY.

—— *United States. See* BRYANT.

History and Principles of Weaving by Hand and by Power. With several hundred Illustrations. By ALFRED BARLOW. Royal 8vo, cloth extra, 1*l.* 5*s.* Second Edition.

Hitchman (*Francis*) *Public Life of the Right Hon. Benjamin* Disraeli, Earl of Beaconsfield. New Edition, with Portrait. Crown 8vo, 3*s.* 6*d.*

Holmes (*O. W.*) *The Poetical Works of Oliver Wendell Holmes.* In 2 vols., 18mo, exquisitely printed, and chastely bound in limp cloth, gilt tops, 10*s.* 6*d.*

Hoppus (*F. D.*) *Riverside Papers.* 2 vols., 12*s.*

Hovgaard (*A.*) See " Nordenskiöld's Voyage." 8vo, 21*s.*

How I Crossed Africa : from the Atlantic to the Indian Ocean, Through Unknown Countries ; Discovery of the Great Zambesi Affluents, &c.—Vol. I., The King's Rifle. Vol. II., The Coillard Family. By Major SERPA PINTO. With 24 full-page and 118 half-page and smaller Illustrations, 13 small Maps, and 1 large one. 2 vols., demy 8vo, cloth extra, 42*s.*

How to get Strong and how to Stay so. By WILLIAM BLAIKIE. A Manual of Rational, Physical, Gymnastic, and other Exercises. With Illustrations, small post 8vo, 5*s.*

Hugo (*Victor*) "*Ninety-Three.*" Illustrated. Crown 8vo, 6*s.*

—— *Toilers of the Sea.* Crown 8vo. Illustrated, 6*s.* ; fancy boards, 2*s.* ; cloth, 2*s.* 6*d.* ; on large paper with all the original Illustrations, 10*s.* 6*d.*

—— *and his Times.* Translated from the French of A. BARBOU by ELLEN E. FREWER. 120 Illustrations, many of them from designs by Victor Hugo himself. Super-royal 8vo, cloth extra, 24*s.*

—— *See* " History of a Crime."

Hundred Greatest Men (The). 8 portfolios, 21*s.* each, or 4 vols., half-morocco, gilt edges, 12 guineas, containing 15 to 20 Portraits each. See below.

"Messrs. SAMPSON LOW & Co. are about to issue an important 'International' work, entitled, 'THE HUNDRED GREATEST MEN;' being the Lives and Portraits of the 100 Greatest Men of History, divided into Eight Classes, each Class to form a Monthly Quarto Volume. The Introductions to the volumes are to be written by recognized authorities on the different subjects, the English contributors being DEAN STANLEY, Mr. MATTHEW ARNOLD, Mr. FROUDE, and Professor MAX MÜLLER: in Germany, Professor HELMHOLTZ; in France, MM. TAINE and RENAN; and in America, Mr. EMERSON. The Portraits are to be Reproductions from fine and rare Steel Engravings."—*Academy.*

Hygiene and Public Health (A Treatise on). Edited by A. H. BUCK, M.D. Illustrated by numerous Wood Engravings. In 2 royal 8vo vols., cloth, One guinea each.

Hymnal Companion to Book of Common Prayer. See BICKERSTETH.

ILLUSTRATED Text-Books of Art-Education. Edited by EDWARD J. POYNTER, R.A. Each Volume contains numerous Illustrations, and is strongly bound for the use of Students, price 5*s.* The Volumes now ready are:—

PAINTING.

Classic and Italian. By PERCY R. HEAD. German, Flemish, and Dutch.	French and Spanish. English and American.

ARCHITECTURE.

Classic and Early Christian.
Gothic and Renaissance. By T. ROGER SMITH.

SCULPTURE.

Antique: Egyptian and Greek.	Renaissance and Modern.

Italian Sculptors of the 14th and 15th Centuries.

ORNAMENT.

Decoration in Colour.	Architectural Ornament.

Illustrated Dictionary (An) of Words used in Art and Archæology. Explaining Terms frequently used in Works on Architecture, Arms, Bronzes, Christian Art, Colour, Costume, Decoration, Devices, Emblems, Heraldry, Lace, Personal Ornaments, Pottery, Painting, Sculpture, &c., with their Derivations. By J. W. MOLLETT, B.A., Officier de l'Instruction Publique (France); Author of "Life of Rembrandt," &c. Illustrated with 600 Wood Engravings. Small 4to, strongly bound in cloth, 15*s.*

In my Indian Garden. By PHIL ROBINSON, Author of "Under the Punkah." With a Preface by EDWIN ARNOLD, M.A., C.S.I., &c. Crown 8vo, limp cloth, 4th Edition, 3*s.* 6*d.*

Irving (Washington). Complete Library Edition of his **Works** in 27 Vols., Copyright, Unabridged, and with the Author's Latest Revisions, called the "Geoffrey Crayon" Edition, handsomely printed in large square 8vo, on superfine laid paper, and each volume, of about 500 pages, will be fully Illustrated. 12*s.* 6*d.* per vol. *See also* "Little Britain."

———————————— ("American Men of Letters.") 2*s.* 6*d.*

JAMES (C.) Curiosities of Law and Lawyers. 8vo, 7*s.* 6*d.*

Johnson (O.) William Lloyd Garrison and his Times. Crown 8vo, 12*s.* 6*d.*

Jones (Major) The Emigrants' Friend. A Complete Guide to the United States. New Edition. 2*s.* 6*d.*

KEMPIS (Thomas à) Daily Text-Book. Square 16mo, 2*s.* 6*d.*; interleaved as a Birthday Book, 3*s.* 6*d.*

Kingston (W. H. G.). See "Snow-Shoes," "Child of the Cavern," "Two Supercargoes," "With Axe and Rifle," "Begum's Fortune," "Heir of Kilfinnan," "Dick Cheveley." Each vol., with very numerous Illustrations, square crown 16mo, gilt edges, 7*s.* 6*d.*; plainer binding, plain edges, 5*s.*

LADY Silverdale's Sweetheart. 6*s.* *See* BLACK.

Lanier. See "Boy's Froissart," "King Arthur," &c.

Lansdell (H.) Through Siberia. 2 vols., demy 8vo, 30*s.*; New Edition, very numerous illustrations, 8vo, 15*s.*

Larden (W.) School Course on Heat. Illustrated, crown 8vo, 5*s.*

Lathrop (G. P.) In the Distance. 2 vols., crown 8vo, 21*s.*

Lectures on Architecture. By E. VIOLLET-LE-DUC. Translated by BENJAMIN BUCKNALL, Architect. With 33 Steel Plates and 200 Wood Engravings. Super-royal 8vo, leather back, gilt top, with complete Index, 2 vols., 3*l.* 3*s.*

Leyland (R. W.) A Holiday in South Africa. Crown 8vo 12*s.* 6*d.*

Library of Religious Poetry. A Collection of the Best Poems of all Ages and Tongues. Edited by PHILIP SCHAFF, D.D., LL.D., and ARTHUR GILMAN, M.A. Royal 8vo, 1036 pp., cloth extra, gilt edges, 21*s.*; re-issue in cheaper binding, 10*s.* 6*d.*

Lindsay (W. S.) History of Merchant Shipping and Ancient Commerce. Over 150 Illustrations, Maps, and Charts. In 4 vols., demy 8vo, cloth extra. Vols. 1 and 2, 11*s.* ; vols. 3 and 4, 14*s.* each. 4 vols. complete for 50*s.*

Little Britain; together with *The Spectre Bridegroom,* and *A* Legend of Sleepy Hollow. By WASHINGTON IRVING. An entirely New *Edition de luxe,* specially suitable for Presentation. Illustrated by 120 very fine Engravings on Wood, by Mr. J. D. COOPER. Designed by Mr. CHARLES O. MURRAY. Re-issue, square crown 8vo, cloth, 6*s.*

Long (Mrs. W. H. C.) Peace and War in the Transvaal. 12mo, 3*s.* 6*d.*

Lorna Doone. 6*s.,* 31*s.* 6*d.,* 35*s.* See " Blackmore."

Low's Select Novelets. Small post 8vo, cloth extra, 3*s.* 6*d.* each.

> **Friends : a Duet.** By E. S. PHELPS, Author of "The Gates Ajar."
> **Baby Rue : Her Adventures and Misadventures, her Friends** and her Enemies. By CHARLES M. CLAY.
> **The Story of Helen Troy.**
> "A pleasant book."—*Truth.*
> **The Clients of Dr. Bernagius.** From the French of LUCIEN BIART, by Mrs. CASHEL HOEY.
> **The Undiscovered Country.** By W. D. HOWELLS.
> **A Gentleman of Leisure.** By EDGAR FAWCETT.

Low's Standard Library of Travel and Adventure. Crown 8vo, bound uniformly in cloth extra, price 7*s.* 6*d.,* except where price is given.

> 1. **The Great Lone Land.** By Major W. F. BUTLER, C.B.
> 2. **The Wild North Land.** By Major W. F. BUTLER, C.B.
> 3. **How I found Livingstone.** By H. M. STANLEY.
> 4. **Through the Dark Continent.** By H. M. STANLEY. 12*s.* 6*d.*
> 5. **The Threshold of the Unknown Region.** By C. R. MARKHAM. (4th Edition, with Additional Chapters, 10*s.* 6*d.*)
> 6. **Cruise of the Challenger.** By W. J. J. SPRY, R.N.
> 7. **Burnaby's On Horseback through Asia Minor.** 10*s.* 6*d.*
> 8. **Schweinfurth's Heart of Africa.** 2 vols., 15*s.*
> 9. **Marshall's Through America.**

Low's Standard Novels. Crown 8vo, 6s. each, cloth extra.

Work. A Story of Experience. By LOUISA M. ALCOTT.
A Daughter of Heth. By W. BLACK.
In Silk Attire. By W. BLACK.
Kilmeny. A Novel. By W. BLACK.
Lady Silverdale's Sweetheart. By W. BLACK.
Sunrise. By W. BLACK.
Three Feathers. By WILLIAM BLACK.
Alice Lorraine. By R. D. BLACKMORE.
Christowell, a Dartmoor Tale. By R. D. BLACKMORE.
Clara Vaughan. By R. D. BLACKMORE.
Cradock Nowell. By R. D. BLACKMORE.
Cripps the Carrier. By R. D. BLACKMORE.
Erema; or, My Father's Sin. By R. D. BLACKMORE.
Lorna Doone. By R. D. BLACKMORE.
Mary Anerley. By R. D. BLACKMORE.
An English Squire. By Miss COLERIDGE.
Mistress Judith. A Cambridgeshire Story. By C. C. FRASER-
TYTLER.
A Story of the Dragonnades; or, Asylum Christi. By the Rev.
E. GILLIAT, M.A.
A Laodicean. By THOMAS HARDY.
Far from the Madding Crowd. By THOMAS HARDY.
The Hand of Ethelberta. By THOMAS HARDY.
The Trumpet Major. By THOMAS HARDY.
Three Recruits. By JOSEPH HATTON.
A Golden Sorrow. By Mrs. CASHEL HOEY. New Edition.
Out of Court. By Mrs. CASHEL HOEY.
History of a Crime: The Story of the Coup d'État. VICTOR
HUGO.
Ninety-Three. By VICTOR HUGO. Illustrated.
Adela Cathcart. By GEORGE MAC DONALD.
Guild Court. By GEORGE MAC DONALD.
Mary Marston. By GEORGE MAC DONALD.
Stephen Archer. New Edition of "Gifts." By GEORGE MAC
DONALD.
The Vicar's Daughter. By GEORGE MAC DONALD.
Weighed and Wanting. By GEORGE MAC DONALD.
[In the Press.
Diane. By Mrs. MACQUOID.
Elinor Dryden. By Mrs. MACQUOID.
My Lady Greensleeves. By HELEN MATHERS.
John Holdsworth. By W. CLARK RUSSELL.
A Sailor's Sweetheart. By W. CLARK RUSSELL.
Wreck of the Grosvenor. By W. CLARK RUSSELL.
The Afghan Knife. By R. A. STERNDALE.
My Wife and I. By Mrs. BEECHER STOWE.
Poganuc People, Their Loves and Lives. By Mrs. B. STOWE.
Ben Hur: a Tale of the Christ. By LEW. WALLACE.

Low's Handbook to the Charities of London (Annual). Edited and revised to date by C. MACKESON, F.S.S., Editor of "A Guide to the Churches of London and its Suburbs," &c. Paper, 1s.; cloth, 1s. 6d.

M^{AC} *DONALD (G.) Orts.* Small post 8vo, 6s.

—— See also "Low's Standard Novels."

Macgregor (John) "Rob Roy" on the Baltic. 3rd Edition, small post 8vo, 2s. 6d.; cloth, gilt edges, 3s. 6d.

—— *A Thousand Miles in the "Rob Roy" Canoe.* 11th Edition, small post 8vo, 2s. 6d.; cloth, gilt edges, 3s. 6d.

—— *Description of the "Rob Roy" Canoe,* with Plans, &c., 1s.

—— *The Voyage Alone in the Yawl "Rob Roy."* New Edition, thoroughly revised, with additions, small post 8vo, 5s.; boards, 2s. 6d.

Macquoid (Mrs.). See LOW'S STANDARD NOVELS.

Magazine. See HARPER, UNION JACK, THE ETCHER, MEN OF MARK.

*Magyarland. A Narrative of Travels through the Snowy Car-*pathians, and Great Alföld of the Magyar. By a Fellow of the Carpathian Society (Diploma of 1881), and Author of "The Indian Alps." 2 vols., 8vo, cloth extra, with about 120 Woodcuts from the Author's own sketches and drawings, 38s.

Manitoba: its History, Growth, and Present Position. By the Rev. Professor BRYCE, Principal of Manitoba College, Winnipeg. Crown 8vo, with Illustrations and Maps, 7s. 6d.

Markham (C. R.) The Threshold of the Unknown Region. Crown 8vo, with Four Maps, 4th Edition. Cloth extra, 10s. 6d.

Markham (C. R.) War between Peru and Chili, 1879-1881. Crown 8vo, with four Maps. [*In preparation.*]

Marshall (W. G.) Through America. New Edition. 8vo, with about 100 Illustrations, 21s.

Maxwell (W. H.) Life of the Duke of Wellington. d Spinning

Maury (Commander) Physical Geography of the Sea, and its Meteorology. Being a Reconstruction and Enlargement of his former Work, with Charts and Diagrams. New Edition, crown 8vo, 6s.

Memoirs of Madame de Rémusat, 1802—1808. By her Grandson, M. PAUL DE RÉMUSAT, Senator. Translated by Mrs. CASHEL HOEY and Mr. JOHN LILLIE. 4th Edition, cloth extra. This work was written by Madame de Rémusàt during the time she was living on the most intimate terms with the Empress Josephine, and is full of revelations respecting the private life of Bonaparte, and of men and politics of the first years of the century. Revelations which have already created a great sensation in Paris. 8vo, 2 vols., 32s.

—— *See also* " Selection."

Ménus (366, *one for each day of the year*). Each Ménu is given in French and English, with the recipe for making every dish mentioned. Translated from the French of COUNT BRISSE, by Mrs. MATTHEW CLARKE. Crown 8vo, 5s.

Men of Mark: a Gallery of Contemporary Portraits of the most Eminent Men of the Day taken from Life, especially for this publication, price 1s. 6d. monthly. Vols. I. to VII., handsomely bound, cloth, gilt edges, 25s. each.

Mendelssohn Family (The), 1729—1847. From Letters and Journals. Translated from the German of SEBASTIAN HENSEL. 3rd Edition, 2 vols., demy 8vo, 30s.

Michael Strogoff. See VERNE.

Mitford (Miss). See " Our Village."

Modern Etchings of Celebrated Paintings. 4to, 31s. 6d.

Mollett (F. W.) Illustrated Dictionary of Words used in Art and Archæology. Small 4to, 15s.

Morley (H.) English Literature in the Reign of Victoria. The 2000th volume of the Tauchnitz Collection of Authors. 18mo, 2s. 6d.

Music. See " Great Musicians."

NARRATIVES of State Trials in the Nineteenth Century. First Period: From the Union with Ireland to the Death of George IV., 1801—1830. By G. LATHOM BROWNE, of the Middle Temple, Barrister-at-Law. 2nd Edition, 2 vols., crown 8vo, cloth, 26s.

Nature and Functions of Art (The); and more especially of Architecture. By LEOPOLD EIDLITZ. Medium 8vo, cloth, 21s.

Naval Brigade in South Africa (The). By HENRY F. NORBURY, C.B., R.N. Crown 8vo, cloth extra, 10s. 6d.

New Child's Play (*A*). Sixteen Drawings by E. V. B. Beautifully printed in colours, 4to, cloth extra, 12s. 6d.

Newfoundland. By FRASER RAE. See "From Newfoundland."

New Novels. Crown 8vo, cloth, 10s. 6d. per vol. :—
The Granvilles. By the Hon. E. TALBOT. 3 vols.
One of Us. By E. RANDOLPH.
Weighed and Wanting. By GEORGE MAC DONALD. 3 vols.
Castle Warlock. By GEORGE MAC DONALD. 3 vols.
Under the Downs. By E. GILLIAT. 3 vols.
A Stranger in a Strange Land. By LADY CLAY. 3 vols.
The Heart of Erin. By Miss OWENS BLACKBURN. 3 vols.
A Chelsea Householder. 3 vols.
Two on a Tower. By THOMAS HARDY. 3 vols.
The Lady Maud. By W. CLARK RUSSELL. 3 vols.

Nice and Her Neighbours. By the Rev. CANON HOLE, Author of "A Book about Roses," "A Little Tour in Ireland," &c. Small 4to, with numerous choice Illustrations, 12s. 6d.

Noah's Ark. A Contribution to the Study of Unnatural History. By PHIL ROBINSON. Small post 8vo, 12s. 6d.

Noble Words and Noble Deeds. From the French of E. MULLER. Containing many Full-page Illustrations by PHILIPPOTEAUX. Square imperial 16mo, cloth extra, 7s. 6d. ; plainer binding, plain edges, 5s.

Nordenskiöld's Voyage around Asia and Europe. A Popular Account of the North-East Passage of the "Vega." By Lieut. A. HOVGAARD, of the Royal Danish Navy, and member of the "Vega" Expedition. 8vo, with about 50 Illustrations and 3 Maps, 21s.

Nordhoff (C.) California, for Health, Pleasure, and Residence. New Edition, 8vo, with Maps and Illustrations, 12s. 6d.

Nothing to Wear ; and Two Millions. By W. A. BUTLER. New Edition. Small post 8vo, in stiff coloured wrapper, 1s.

Nursery Playmates (*Prince of*). 217 Coloured Pictures for Children by eminent Artists. Folio, in coloured boards, 6s.

*O*FF *to the Wilds: A Story for Boys.* By G. MANVILLE FENN. Profusely Illustrated. Crown 8vo, 7s. 6d.

Old-Fashioned Girl. See ALCOTT.

On Horseback through Asia Minor. By Capt. FRED BURNABY. 2 vols., 8vo, 38s. Cheaper Edition, crown 8vo, 10s. 6d.

Our Little Ones in Heaven. Edited by the Rev. H. ROBBINS. With Frontispiece after Sir JOSHUA REYNOLDS. Fcap., cloth extra, New Edition—the 3rd, with Illustrations, 5s.

Our Village. By MARY RUSSELL MITFORD. Illustrated with Frontispiece Steel Engraving, and 12 full-page and 157 smaller Cuts. Crown 4to, cloth, gilt edges, 21*s.*; cheaper binding, 10*s.* 6*d.*

Our Woodland Trees. By F. G. HEATH. Large post 8vo, cloth, gilt edges, uniform with "Fern World" and "Fern Paradise," by the same Author. 8 Coloured Plates (showing leaves of every British Tree) and 20 Woodcuts, cloth, gilt edges, 12*s.* 6*d.* New Edition. About 600 pages.

Outlines of Ornament in all Styles. A Work of Reference for the Architect, Art Manufacturer, Decorative Artist, and Practical Painter. By W. and G. A. AUDSLEY, Fellows of the Royal Institute of British Architects. Only a limited number have been printed and the stones destroyed. Small folio, 60 plates, with introductory text, cloth gilt, 31*s.* 6*d.*

PALLISER (Mrs.) A History of Lace, from the Earliest Period. A New and Revised Edition, with additional cuts and text, upwards of 100 Illustrations and coloured Designs. 1 vol., 8vo, 1*l.* 1*s.*

—— *Historic Devices, Badges, and War Cries.* 8vo, 1*l.* 1*s.*

—— *The China Collector's Pocket Companion.* With upwards of 1000 Illustrations of Marks and Monograms. 2nd Edition, with Additions. Small post 8vo, limp cloth, 5*s.*

Pathways of Palestine: a Descriptive Tour through the Holy Land. By the Rev. CANON TRISTRAM. Illustrated with 44 permanent Photographs. (The Photographs are large, and most perfect Specimens of the Art.) Vols. I. and II., folio, gilt edges, 31*s.* 6*d.* each.

Peasant Life in the West of England. By FRANCIS GEORGE HEATH, Author of "Sylvan Spring," "The Fern World." Crown 8vo, 400 pp. (with Facsimile of Autograph Letter from Lord Beaconsfield to the Author, written December 28, 1880), 10*s.* 6*d.*

Petites Leçons de Conversation et de Grammaire: Oral and Conversational Method ; the most Useful Topics of Conversation. By F. JULIEN. Cloth, 3*s.* 6*d.*

Photography (History and Handbook of). See TISSANDIER.

Physical Treatise on Electricity and Magnetism. By J. E. H. GORDON, B.A. With about 200 coloured, full-page, and other Illustrations. 2 vols., 8vo. New Edition. [*In preparation.*

Poems of the Inner Life. Chiefly from Modern Authors. Small 8vo, 5*s.*

Poganuc People: their Loves and Lives. By Mrs. BEECHER STOWE. Crown 8vo, cloth, 6*s.*

Polar Expeditions. *See* KOLDEWEY, MARKHAM, MACGAHAN, NARES, and NORDENSKIÖLD.

Poynter (Edward J., R.A.). *See* "Illustrated Text-books."

Prudence: a Story of Æsthetic London. By LUCY E. LILLIE. Small 8vo, 5*s.*

Publishers' Circular (The), and General Record of British and Foreign Literature. Published on the 1st and 15th of every Month, 3*d.*

Pyrenees (The). By HENRY BLACKBURN. With 100 Illustrations by GUSTAVE DORÉ, corrected to 1881. Crown 8vo, 7*s.* 6*d.*

*R*AE *(F.) Newfoundland.* See "From."

Redford (G.) Ancient Sculpture. Crown 8vo, 5*s.*

Reid (T. W.) Land of the Bey. Post 8vo, 10*s.* 6*d.*

Rémusat (Madame de). *See* "Memoirs of," "Selection."

Richter (Jean Paul). *The Literary Works of Leonardo da* Vinci. Containing his Writings on Painting, Sculpture, and Architecture, his Philosophical Maxims, Humorous Writings, and Miscellaneous Notes on Personal Events, on his Contemporaries, on Literature, &c. ; for the first time published from Autograph Manuscripts. By J. P. RICHTER, Ph.Dr., Hon. Member of the Royal and Imperial Academy of Rome, &c. 2 vols., imperial 8vo, containing about 200 Drawings in Autotype Reproductions, and numerous other Illustrations. Price Eight Guineas to Subscribers. After publication the price will be Twelve Guineas.

—— *Italian Art in the National Gallery.* 4to. Illustrated. Cloth gilt, 2*l.* 2*s.*; half-morocco, uncut, 2*l.* 12*s.* 6*d.*

Robinson (Phil). See "In my Indian Garden," "Under the Punkah," "Noah's Ark," "Sinners and Saints."

Rose (F.) Complete Practical Machinist. New Edition, 12mo, 12*s.* 6*d.*

Rose Library (The). Popular Literature of all Countries. Each volume, 1*s.*; cloth, 2*s.* 6*d.* Many of the Volumes are Illustrated—
Little Women. By LOUISA M. ALCOTT.
Little Women Wedded. Forming a Sequel to "Little Women."
Little Men. By L. M. ALCOTT. Dble. vol., 2*s.*; cloth gilt, 3*s.* 6*d.*
An Old-Fashioned Girl. By LOUISA M. ALCOTT. Double vol., 2*s.*; cloth, 3*s.* 6*d.*
Work. A Story of Experience. By L. M. ALCOTT.
Beginning Again. Sequel to "Work." By L. M. ALCOTT.
Stowe (Mrs. H. B.) The Pearl of Orr's Island.
—— **The Minister's Wooing.**

Rose Library (*continued*):—

Stowe (Mrs. H. B.) We and our Neighbours. Double vol., 2*s*
cloth, 3*s*. 6*d*.

—— **My Wife and I.** Double vol., 2*s*.; cloth gilt, 3*s*. 6*d*.

Hans Brinker; or, the Silver Skates. By Mrs. DODGE.

My Study Windows. By J. R. LOWELL.

The Guardian Angel. By OLIVER WENDELL HOLMES.

My Summer in a Garden. By C. D. WARNER.

Dred. Mrs. BEECHER STOWE. Dble. vol., 2*s*.; cloth gilt, 3*s*. 6*d*.

Farm Ballads. By WILL CARLETON.

Farm Festivals. By WILL CARLETON.

Farm Legends. By WILL CARLETON.

The Clients of Dr. Bernagius. 2 parts, 1*s*. each.

The Undiscovered Country. By W. D. HOWELLS.

Baby Rue. By C. M. CLAY.

The Rose in Bloom. By L. M. ALCOTT. 2*s*.; cloth gilt, 3*s*. 6*d*.

Eight Cousins. By L. M. ALCOTT. 2*s*.; cloth gilt, 3*s*. 6*d*.

Under the Lilacs. By L. M. ALCOTT. 2*s*.; cloth gilt, 3*s*. 6*d*.

Silver Pitchers. By LOUISA M. ALCOTT.

Jemmy's Cruise in the "Pinafore," and other Tales. By
LOUISA M. ALCOTT. 2*s*.; cloth gilt, 3*s*. 6*d*.

Jack and Jill. By LOUISA M. ALCOTT. 2*s*.; cloth gilt, 3*s*. 6*d*.

Hitherto. By the Author of the "Gayworthys." 2 vols., 1*s*. each.

Friends: a Duet. By E. STUART PHELPS.

A Gentleman of Leisure. A Novel. By EDGAR FAWCETT.

The Story of Helen Troy.

Round the Yule Log: Norwegian Folk and Fairy Tales.
Translated from the Norwegian of P. CHR. ASBJÖRNSEN. With 100
Illustrations after drawings by Norwegian Artists, and an Introduction
by E. W. Gosse. Imperial 16mo, cloth extra, gilt edges, 7*s*. 6*d*.

Rousselet (Louis) Son of the Constable of France. Small post
8vo, numerous Illustrations, 5*s*.

—— *The Drummer Boy: a Story of the Days of Washington.*
Small post 8vo, numerous Illustrations, 5*s*.

Russell (W. Clark) The Lady Maud. 3 vols., crown 8vo,
31*s*. 6*d*.

—— *See also* LOW'S STANDARD NOVELS *and* WRECK.

Russell (W. H., LL.D.) Hesperothen: Notes from the Western
World. A Record of a Ramble through part of the United States,
Canada, and the Far West, in the Spring and Summer of 1881. By
W. II. RUSSELL, LL.D. 2 vols., crown 8vo, cloth, 24*s*.

—— *The Tour of the Prince of Wales in India.* By
W. H. RUSSELL, LL.D. Fully Illustrated by SYDNEY P. HALL,
M.A. Super-royal 8vo, cloth extra, gilt edges, 52*s*. 6*d*.; Large
Paper Edition, 84*s*.

Russian Literature. See "Turner."

S*AINTS and their Symbols : A Companion in the Churches*
and Picture Galleries of Europe. With Illustrations. Royal 16mo,
cloth extra, 3*s.* 6*d.*

Scherr (Prof. F.) History of English Literature. Translated
from the German. Crown 8vo, 8*s.* 6*d.*

Schuyler (Eugène). The Life of Peter the Great. By EUGÈNE
SCHUYLER, Author of "Turkestan." 2 vols., demy 8vo.
[In preparation.

Scott (Leader) Renaissance of Art in. Italy. 4to, 31*s.* 6*d.*

Selection from the Letters of Madame de Rémusat to her Husband
and Son, from 1804 to 1813. From the French, by Mrs. CASHEL
HOEY and Mr. JOHN LILLIE. In 1 vol., demy 8vo (uniform with
the "Memoirs of Madame de Rémusat," 2 vols.), cloth extra, 16*s.*

Senior (Nassau W.) Conversations and Journals in Egypt and
Malta. 2 vols., 8vo, 24*s.*
These volumes contain conversations with SAID PASHA, ACHIM BEY,
HEKEKYAN BEY, the Patriarch, M. DE LESSEPS, M. ST. HILAIRE,
Sir FREDERICK BRUCE, Sir ADRIAN DINGLI, and many other remark-
able people.

Seonee : Sporting in the Satpura Range of Central India, and in
the Valley of the Nerbudda. By R. A. STERNDALE, F.R.G.S. 8vo,
with numerous Illustrations, 21*s.*

Shadbolt (S.) The Afghan Campaigns of 1878—1880. By
SYDNEY SHADBOLT, Joint Author of "The South African Campaign
of 1879." 2 vols., royal quarto, cloth extra, 3*l.* 3*s.*

Shooting : its Appliances, Practice, and Purpose. By JAMES
DALZIEL DOUGALL, F.S.A., F.Z.A., Author of "Scottish Field
Sports," &c. New Edition, revised with additions. Crown 8vo,
cloth extra, 7*s.* 6*d.*
"The book is admirable in every way. . . . . We wish it every success."—*Globe.*
"A very complete treatise. . . . . Likely to take high rank as an authority on
shooting."—*Daily News.*

Sikes (Wirt). Rambles and Studies in Old South Wales. With
numerous Illustrations. Demy 8vo, 18*s.*

Silent Hour (The). See "Gentle Life Series."

Silver Sockets (The) ; and other Shadows of Redemption.
Eighteen Sermons preached in Christ Church, Hampstead, by the
Rev. C. H. WALLER. Small post 8vo, cloth, 6*s.*

Sinners and Saints : a Tour across the United States of
America, and Round them. By PHIL ROBINSON. *[In the Press.*

Sir Roger de Coverley. Re-imprinted from the "Spectator."
With 125 Woodcuts, and steel Frontispiece specially designed and
engraved for the Work. Small fcap. 4to, 6*s.*

Smith (G.) Assyrian Explorations and Discoveries. By the late
GEORGE SMITH. Illustrated by Photographs and Woodcuts. Demy
8vo, 6th Edition, 18s.

———— *The Chaldean Account of Genesis.* By the late G.
SMITH, of the Department of Oriental Antiquities, British Museum.
With many Illustrations. Demy 8vo, cloth extra, 6th Edition, 16s.
An entirely New Edition, completely revised and re-written by the
Rev. PROFESSOR SAYCE, Queen's College, Oxford. Demy 8vo, 18s.

Smith (J. Moyr). See "Ancient Greek Female Costume."

Snow-Shoes and Canoes; or, the Adventures of a Fur-Hunter
in the Hudson's Bay Territory. By W. H. G. KINGSTON. 2nd
Edition. With numerous Illustrations. Square crown 8vo, cloth
extra, gilt edges, 7s. 6d. ; plainer binding, 5s.

South African Campaign, 1879 *(The).* Compiled by J. P.
MACKINNON (formerly 72nd Highlanders), and S. H. SHADBOLT ;
and dedicated, by permission, to Field-Marshal H.R.H. The Duke
of Cambridge. Containing a portrait and biography of every officer
killed in the campaign. 4to, handsomely bound in cloth extra, 2l. 10s.

South Kensington Museum. Vol. II., 21s.

Stack (E.) Six Months in Persia. 2 vols., crown 8vo, 24s.

Stanley (H. M.) How I Found Livingstone. Crown 8vo, cloth
extra, 7s. 6d. ; large Paper Edition, 10s. 6d.

———— *"My Kalulu," Prince, King, and Slave.* A Story
from Central Africa. Crown 8vo, about 430 pp., with numerous graphic
Illustrations, after Original Designs by the Author. Cloth, 7s. 6d.

———— *Coomassie and Magdala.* A Story of Two British
Campaigns in Africa. Demy 8vo, with Maps and Illustrations, 16s.

———— *Through the Dark Continent.* Cheaper Edition,
crown 8vo, 12s. 6d.

State Trials. See "Narratives."

Stenhouse (Mrs.) An Englishwoman in Utah. Crown 8vo, 2s. 6d.

Stoker (Bram) Under the Sunset. Crown 8vo, 6s.

Story without an End. From the German of Carové, by the late
Mrs. SARAH T. AUSTIN. Crown 4to, with 15 Exquisite Drawings
by E. V. B., printed in Colours in Fac-simile of the original Water
Colours ; and numerous other Illustrations. New Edition, 7s. 6d.

———— square 4to, with Illustrations by HARVEY. 2s. 6d.

Stowe (Mrs. Beecher) Dred. Cheap Edition, boards, 2s. Cloth,
gilt edges, 3s. 6d.

Stowe (Mrs Beecher) Footsteps of the Master. With Illustrations and red borders. Small post 8vo, cloth extra, 6s.

———— *Geography*, with 60 Illustrations. Square cloth, 4s. 6d.

———— *Little Foxes.* Cheap Edition, 1s.; Library Edition, 4s. 6d.

———— *Betty's Bright Idea.* 1s.

———— *My Wife and I; or, Harry Henderson's History.* Small post 8vo, cloth extra, 6s.*

———— *Minister's Wooing.* 5s.; Copyright Series, 1s. 6d.; cl., 2s.*

———— *Old Town Folk.* 6s.; Cheap Edition, 2s. 6d.

———— *Old Town Fireside Stories.* Cloth extra, 3s. 6d.

———— *Our Folks at Poganuc.* 6s.

———— *We and our Neighbours.* 1 vol., small post 8vo, 6s. Sequel to "My Wife and I."*

———— *Pink and White Tyranny.* Small post 8vo, 3s. 6d. Cheap Edition, 1s. 6d. and 2s.

———— *Queer Little People.* 1s.; cloth, 2s.

———— *Chimney Corner.* 1s.; cloth, 1s. 6d.

———— *The Pearl of Orr's Island.* Crown 8vo, 5s.*

———— *Woman in Sacred History.* Illustrated with 15 Chromo-lithographs and about 200 pages of Letterpress. Demy 4to, cloth extra, gilt edges, 25s.

Student's French Examiner. By F. JULIEN, Author of "Petites Leçons de Conversation et de Grammaire." Square cr. 8vo, cloth, 2s.

Studies in the Theory of Descent. By Dr. AUG. WEISMANN, Professor in the University of Freiburg. Translated and edited by RAPHAEL MELDOLA, F.C.S., Secretary of the Entomological Society of London. Part I.—"On the Seasonal Dimorphism of Butterflies," containing Original Communications by Mr. W. H. EDWARDS, of Coalburgh. With two Coloured Plates. Price of Part I. (to Subscribers for the whole work only), 8s.; Part II. (6 coloured plates), 16s.; Part III., 6s. Complete, 2 vols., 40s.

Surgeon's Handbook on the Treatment of Wounded in War. By Dr. FRIEDRICH ESMARCH, Surgeon-General to the Prussian Army. Numerous Coloured Plates and Illustrations, 8vo, strongly bound, 1l. 8s.

* *See also* Rose Library.

Sylvan Spring. By FRANCIS GEORGE HEATH. Illustrated by
12 Coloured Plates, drawn by F. E. HULME, F.L.S., Artist and
Author of "Familiar Wild Flowers;" by 16 full-page, and more than
100 other Wood Engravings. Large post 8vo, cloth, gilt edges, 12s. 6d.

TAHITI. By Lady BRASSEY, Author of the "Voyage of
the Sunbeam." With 31 Autotype Illustrations after Photos. by
Colonel STUART-WORTLEY. Fcap. 4to, very tastefully bound, 21s.

Taine (H. A.) "Les Origines de la France Contemporaine."
Translated by JOHN DURAND.
 Vol. 1. **The Ancient Regime.** Demy 8vo, cloth, 16s.
 Vol. 2. **The French Revolution.** Vol. 1. do.
 Vol. 3. **Do.** do. Vol. 2. do.

Tauchnitz's English Editions of German Authors. Each
volume, cloth flexible, 2s. ; or sewed, 1s. 6d. (Catalogues post free
on application.)

———— (B.) *German and English Dictionary.* Cloth, 1s. 6d.;
roan, 2s.

———— *French and English Dictionary.* Paper, 1s. 6d.;
cloth, 2s.; roan, 2s. 6d.

———— *Italian and English Dictionary.* Paper, 1s. 6d.; cloth,
2s. ; roan, 2s. 6d.

———— *Spanish and English.* Paper, 1s. 6d.; cloth, 2s. ; roan,
2s. 6d.

Taylor (W. M.) Paul the Missionary. Crown 8vo, 7s. 6d.

Thausing (Prof.) Preparation of Malt and the Fabrication of
Beer. 8vo, 45s.

Thomas à Kempis. See "Birthday Book."

Thompson (Emma) Wit and Wisdom of Don Quixote. Fcap.
8vo, 3s. 6d.

Thoreau. By SANBORN. (American Men of Letters.) Crown
8vo, 2s. 6d.

Through America ; or, Nine Months in the United States. By
W. G. MARSHALL, M.A. With nearly 100 Woodcuts of Views of
Utah country and the famous Yosemite Valley; The Giant Trees,
New York, Niagara, San Francisco, &c.; containing a full account
of Mormon Life, as noted by the Author during his visits to Salt Lake
City in 1878 and 1879. Demy 8vo, 21s. ; cheap edition, crown 8vo,
7s. 6d.

Through the Dark Continent : The Sources of the Nile ; Around
the Great Lakes, and down the Congo. By H. M. STANLEY.
Cheap Edition, crown 8vo, with some of the Illustrations and Maps,
12s. 6d.

Through Siberia. By the Rev. HENRY LANSDELL. Illustrated
with about 30 Engravings, 2 Route Maps, and Photograph of the
Author, in Fish-skin Costume of the Gilyaks on the Lower Amur.
2 vols., demy 8vo, 30*s.* Cheaper Edition, 1 vol., 15*s.*

Tour of the Prince of Wales in India. *See* RUSSELL.

Trees and Ferns. By F. G. HEATH. Crown 8vo, cloth, gilt
edges, with numerous Illustrations, 3*s.* 6*d.*
    "A charming little volume."—*Land and Water.*

Tristram (Rev. Canon) Pathways of Palestine : A Descriptive
Tour through the Holy Land. First Series. Illustrated by 44 Permanent Photographs. 2 vols., folio, cloth extra, gilt edges, 31*s.* 6*d.*
each.

Turner (Edward) Studies in Russian Literature. (The Author
is English Tutor in the University of St. Petersburgh.) Crown 8vo,
8*s.* 6*d.*

Two Supercargoes (The) ; or, Adventures in Savage Africa.
By W. H. G. KINGSTON. Numerous Full-page Illustrations. Square
imperial 16mo, cloth extra, gilt edges, 7*s.* 6*d.* ; plainer binding, 5*s.*

UNDER the Punkah. By PHIL ROBINSON, Author of "In
my Indian Garden." Crown 8vo, limp cloth, 5*s.*

Union Jack (The). Every Boy's Paper. Edited by G. A.
HENTY and BERNARD HELDMANN. One Penny Weekly, Monthly 6*d.*
Vol. I., New Series.

The Opening Numbers will contain :—
    SERIAL STORIES.

    Straight : Jack Archer's Way in the World. By G. A. HENTY.
    Spiggott's School Days : A Tale of Dr. Merriman's. By CUTHBERT
    BEDE.
    Sweet Flower ; or, Red Skins and Pale Faces. By PERCY B.
    ST. JOHN.
    Under the Meteor Flag. By HARRY COLLINGWOOD.
    The White Tiger. By LOUIS BOUSSENARD. Illustrated.
    A Couple of Scamps. By BERNARD HELDMANN.
    Also a Serial Story by R. MOUNTNEY JEPHSON.

———— Vols. II. and III., 4to, 7*s.* 6*d.* ; gilt edges, 8*s.*

VINCENT (F.) Norsk, Lapp, and Finn. By FRANK
VINCENT, Jun., Author of "The Land of the White Elephant,"
"Through and Through the Tropics," &c. 8vo, cloth, with Frontis-
piece and Map, 12*s.*

Vivian (A. P.) Wanderings in the Western Land. 3rd Edition,
10*s.* 6*d.*

BOOKS BY JULES VERNE.

LARGE CROWN 8vo. — WORKS.	Containing 350 to 600 pp. and from 50 to 100 full-page illustrations.		Containing the whole of the text with some illustrations.	
	In very handsome cloth binding, gilt edges.	In plainer binding, plain edges.	In cloth binding, gilt edges, smaller type.	Coloured Boards.
	s. d.	*s. d.*	*s. d.*	
Twenty Thousand Leagues under the Sea. Part I. Ditto Part II.	10 6	5 0	3 6	2 vols., 1s. each.
Hector Servadac . . .	10 6	5 0	3 6	2 vols., 1s. each.
The Fur Country . . .	10 6	5 0	3 6	2 vols., 1s. each.
From the Earth to the Moon and a Trip round it	10 6	5 0	2 vols., 2s. each.	2 vols., 1s. each.
Michael Strogoff, the Courier of the Czar . .	10 6	5 0	3 6	2 vols., 1s. each.
Dick Sands, the Boy Captain	10 6	5 0	3 6	2 vols., 1s. each.
Five Weeks in a Balloon .	7 6	3 6	2 0	1s. 0d.
Adventures of Three Englishmen and Three Russians	7 6	3 6	2 0	1 0
Around the World in Eighty Days	7 6	3 6	2 0	1 0
A Floating City	7 6	3 6	2 0	1 0
The Blockade Runners .			2 0	1 0
Dr. Ox's Experiment . .			2 0	1 0
Master Zacharius . . .	7 6	3 6		
A Drama in the Air . .			2 0	1 0
A Winter amid the Ice .				
The Survivors of the "Chancellor"	7 6	3 6	2 0	2 vols. 1s. each.
Martin Paz			2 0	1 0
THE MYSTERIOUS ISLAND, 3 vols. :—	22 6	10 6	6 0	3 0
Vol. I. Dropped from the Clouds	7 6	3 6	2 0	1 0
Vol. II. Abandoned . .	7 6	3 6	2 0	1 0
Vol. III. Secret of the Island	7 6	3 6	2 0	1 0
The Child of the Cavern .	7 6	3 6	2 0	1 0
The Begum's Fortune . .	7 6	3 6		
The Tribulations of a Chinaman	7 6	3 6		
THE STEAM HOUSE, 2 vols.:—				
Vol. I. Demon of Cawnpore	7 6			
Vol. II. Tigers and Traitors	7 6			
THE GIANT RAFT, 2 vols.:—				
Vol. I. Eight Hundred Leagues on the Amazon.	7 6			
Vol. II. The Cryptogram	7 6			
Godfrey Morgan . . .	7 6			

CELEBRATED TRAVELS AND TRAVELLERS. 3 vols. Demy 8vo, 600 pp., upwards of 100 full-page illustrations, 12s. 6d. ; gilt edges, 14s. each :—
(1) THE EXPLORATION OF THE WORLD.
(2) THE GREAT NAVIGATORS OF THE EIGHTEENTH CENTURY.
(3) THE GREAT EXPLORERS OF THE NINETEENTH CENTURY.

WAITARUNA: A Story of New Zealand Life. By ALEXANDER BATHGATE, Author of "Colonial Experiences." Crown 8vo, cloth, 5s.

Waller (Rev. C. H.) The Names on the Gates of Pearl, and other Studies. By the Rev. C. H. WALLER, M.A. New Edition. Crown 8vo, cloth extra, 3s. 6d.

—— *A Grammar and Analytical Vocabulary of the Words in* the Greek Testament. Compiled from Brüder's Concordance. For the use of Divinity Students and Greek Testament Classes. By the Rev. C. H. WALLER, M.A. Part I. The Grammar. Small post 8vo, cloth, 2s. 6d. Part II. The Vocabulary, 2s. 6d.

—— *Adoption and the Covenant.* Some Thoughts on Confirmation. Super-royal 16mo, cloth limp, 2s. 6d.

—— *See also* "Silver Sockets."

Wanderings South by East: a Descriptive Record of Four Years of Travel in the less known Countries and Islands of the Southern and Eastern Hemispheres. By WALTER COOTE. 8vo, with very numerous Illustrations and a Map, 21s.

Warner (C. D.) Back-log Studies. Boards, 1s. 6d.; cloth, 2s.

—— *Mummies and Moslems.* 8vo, cloth, 12s.

Washington Irving's Little Britain. Square crown 8vo, 6s.

Weaving. See "History and Principles."

Webster. (American Men of Letters.) 18mo, 2s. 6d.

Weismann (A.) Studies in the Theory of Descent. 2 vols., 8vo, 40s.

Where to Find Ferns. By F. G. HEATH, Author of "The Fern World," &c.; with a Special Chapter on the Ferns round London; Lists of Fern Stations, and Descriptions of Ferns and Fern Habitats throughout the British Isles. Crown 8vo, cloth, price 3s.

White (Rhoda E.) From Infancy to Womanhood. A Book of Instruction for Young Mothers. Crown 8vo, cloth, 10s. 6d.

White (R. G.) England Without and Within. New Edition, crown 8vo, 10s. 6d.

Whittier (J. G.) The King's Missive, and later Poems. 18mo, choice parchment cover, 3s. 6d. This book contains all the Poems written by Mr. Whittier since the publication of "Hazel Blossoms."

—— *The Whittier Birthday Book.* Extracts from the Author's writings, with Portrait and numerous Illustrations. Uniform with the "Emerson Birthday Book." Square 16mo, very choice binding, 3s. 6d.

Wild Flowers of Switzerland. 17 Coloured Plates. 4to.
[*In preparation.*

Williams (H. W.) Diseases of the Eye. 8vo, 21s.

Wills, A Few Hints on Proving, without Professional Assistance.
By a PROBATE COURT OFFICIAL. 5th Edition, revised with Forms
of Wills, Residuary Accounts, &c. Fcap. 8vo, cloth limp, 1s.

Winks (W. E.) Lives of Illustrious Shoemakers. With eight
Portraits. Crown 8vo, 7s. 6d.

With Axe and Rifle on the Western Prairies. By W. H. G.
KINGSTON. With numerous Illustrations, square crown 8vo, cloth
extra, gilt edges, 7s. 6d.; plainer binding, 5s.

Woolsey (C. D., LL.D.) Introduction to the Study of Inter-
national Law; designed as an Aid in Teaching and in Historical
Studies. 5th Edition, demy 8vo, 18s.

Wreck of the Grosvenor. By W. CLARK RUSSELL, Author of
"John Holdsworth, Chief Mate," "A Sailor's Sweetheart," &c. 6s.
Third and Cheaper Edition.

Wright (the late Rev. Henry) The Friendship of God. With
Biographical Preface by the Rev. E. H. BICKERSTETH, Portrait,
&c. Crown 8vo, 6s.

*Y*RIARTE *(Charles) Florence: its History.* Translated by
C. B. PITMAN. Illustrated with 500 Engravings. Large imperial
4to, extra binding, gilt edges, 63s.
History; the Medici; the Humanists; letters; arts; the Renaissance;
illustrious Florentines; Etruscan art; monuments; sculpture; painting.

London:

SAMPSON LOW, MARSTON, SEARLE, & RIVINGTON,

CROWN BUILDINGS, 188, FLEET STREET, E.C.

www.ingramcontent.com/pod-product-compliance
Lightning Source LLC
LaVergne TN
LVHW012205040326
832903LV00003B/133